COURAGE

PERSEVERING IN THE FACE OF FEAR

JON JOHNSTON

Beacon Hill Press of Kansas City
Kansas City, Missouri

ISBN 083-411-7894

Printed in the
United States of America

Cover Design: Paul Franitza
Cover Photo: Tony Stone Images

Library of Congress Cataloging-in-Publication Data

Johnston, Jon.
    Courage / persevering in the face of fear, Jon Johnston.
        p. cm.
    Rev. ed. of: Courage.
    Includes bibliographical references.
    ISBN 0-8341-1789-4 (pbk.)
        1. Courage—Religious aspects—Christianity. I. Johnston, Jon. Courage. II. Title.
BV4647.C75 J64 2000
241'.4—dc21

00-036025

10 9 8 7 6 5 4 3 2 1

To the devoted brothers and sisters of our neighborhood Bible study, whose lives, prayers, and encouragement have provided me with continual courage transfusions.

In memoriam
Michael Scott Fuselier
November 3, 1979—January 31, 2000

CONTENTS

FOREWORD

I once had the privilege of spending time with Mother Teresa in Calcutta. As we walked through the city's streets, I found myself overwhelmed by the poverty and suffering surrounding us. Finally I asked her if she did not grow discouraged facing the enormity of need in Calcutta and in the thousands of other places like it around the world. She responded, "God does not ask me to be successful—He only asked me to be faithful."

There are a thousand and one reasons why Mother Teresa should have given up her work, given in to the suffering. But there's one reason why she continued to be faithful to her calling right up until her death in 1997. Her example provides a marvelous context for this book.

What is this thing we call courage? And what does it mean in the lives of those of us who have accepted Christ? Mother Teresa's words define it as remaining faithful to one's calling despite the odds. In the following pages Jon Johnston expands on this theme and attempts to define this word in the context of a secular world that does not seem to reward real courage, in a secular world full of a thousand and one reasons not to act.

The courage about which he writes, the courage that comes from faithfulness, is a tall order indeed. The courage of faithfulness requires that we struggle against the tide, that we take unpopular stands, that we reach out to those in need. Ultimately it requires that we ignore those many reasons not to act and follow the witness of Christ.

Jesus Christ lived in a world much like ours today, a society that looked dimly upon those who walked with the poor, reached out to the sick, or spoke uncomfortable truths. But He persevered, faithful to His Father's will, a Man of courage. With the same needs continuing to confront us today as faced Christ on earth, the challenge to be courageous remains.

Of course, it's far easier to mouth words than it is to live faithfully. Christians are frequently faced with the temptation to avert their eyes and join the crowd. In Christ we find not only the example of courage but also the power to be forgiven for our failures. Each day offers anew the opportunity to begin again a life of faithfulness—to demonstrate courage.

—*Mark Hatfield*
Former United States Senator from Oregon

A study and leader's guide for this book is
available at the following web site:
www.bhillkc.com

Readers may contact the author at the
following E-mail address:
jjohnsto@pepperdine.edu

INTRODUCTION

I've thought long and hard about the wisdom of writing a book on courage. My conclusion: There are many reasons *not* to do it.

For one thing, books pertaining to this virtue are about as rare as sand on southern California beaches. Also, those who dislike me might use my words to incriminate *me*—pointing out my numerous foibles and shortcomings. But then I ran head-on into some unanticipated situations that called for taking a stand. At first it was exhilarating to follow the urgings of my conscience in the direction of right. Yet I soon experienced some backlash reactions that surprised and distressed me.

Questions began to surface. I asked myself if being courageous, even for noble causes, was really worth the hassle. Wouldn't it have made more sense to sidestep issues, to have gone along with the crowd, to have taken the easy way and let nature take her course? Did I really need to create this self-imposed grief?

All of this prompted me to do some intense soul-searching on the subject of courage—in my own life and in the lives of others.

I had always maintained that cowardice is a killer. It smothers joy, kills hope, annihilates love, and causes the relinquishment of the most noble qualities of character—by default.

By contrast, I had always believed courage to have the opposite effect. It provides fulfillment, gives purpose, and invigorates the soul. And it would seem that most agree. That's why nations give medals to the courageous and name streets after them—while cowards are despised, mocked, and often reduced to shame and remorse.

So why, when faced with some high-pressure situations, was I tempted to second-guess those actions that required a little moral mettle on my part?

To answer these questions, I began to study people around me, and soon I observed many who *were* courageous in quiet, unassuming, unheralded, yet costly ways. This was heartwarming to discover.

At the same time I also noticed what seemed to be a rising tide of cowardice: more and more people refusing to take unpopular, uncompromising stands on crucial issues—especially those that are guaranteed to cause personal discomfort.

The results of increased cowardice can be seen everywhere. People in distress are ignored. Business shenanigans proliferate unchecked. Dangerous criminals get by with no one testifying against them.

Not only did I see people avoiding the call to courage, but also I observed scores of people acting in a truly courageous manner but in situations that were insignificant, petty, and self-serving. They were busy taking bold stands against trivial issues, creating a tempest in a teapot.

How about the Church? I discovered that few of us who claim to be Christ's servants really tackle the causes that are some of the closest to His heart: defending the weak, fighting for justice, countering compromise and deception within the Church.

Just as in the secular society, many of us in the Church shy away completely from taking strong stands. Then there are those of us who get caught up in championing causes of little consequence. In so doing, we give ourselves the illusion that we are being heroic. Theologians argue fine points of doctrine, for instance, while leaving cardinal, biblical principles unclarified. Ecclesiastical bureaucrats constantly jockey for position on their political ladders while seeking to offend no one and glossing over essential inconsistencies. Pastors increasingly adopt the philosophy of growth and growth alone—in numbers, dollars, and buildings.

Finally, instead of seeking ways and means of more closely living out the Master's example, most laypersons seem intent on simply getting by. Their most frequent unasked question is "How much can I get away with and still be considered a Christian?"

All these impressions have driven me to books, to soul-searching, and to my knees. If courage is ebbing away from our nation, and particularly from God's Church, something must be done without delay.

This book claims to do little more than to "put a finger in the dike" and call for help. It's hoped that the readers will pick up the torch and dauntlessly march forward into battle.

To begin with, we must become sensitized to the special need for courage in our day. There's no substitute—and without it, we can have no relief.

With these heartfelt thoughts I hereby contribute "one more grain of sand."

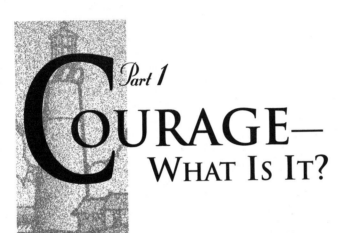

Part 1

COURAGE—
WHAT IS IT?

1

ROUGH AND TOUGH— OR ALL BLUFF?

Mountain climbers connect themselves to one another with a rope to keep the one at the end from going home.
—Charles Swindoll

He has not learned the lesson of life who does not every day surmount a fear.
—Ralph Waldo Emerson

God does not give us an overcoming life. He gives us life as we overcome.
—Oswald Chambers

"I am, don't you ever ever say that word in this house!"

Doro LeBlond, daughter of former United States President George Bush, fired this volley of rebuking words at her son when he used the word "wimp." Why? Because the press had relentlessly accused his grandfather of being one when he was vice president.[1]

World leaders are deeply repulsed by any insinuation of being wimpish. And they have gone to great lengths to cast off the stigma.

Former Mexican President Carlos Salinas aggressively tackled corruption, drugs, and his country's foreign debt, dispelling any labeling of him as a wimp. *Time* magazine tells his story in an article called "Wimp No More."[2]

England's Prince Charles—labeled "the wimpish clown prince" by British tabloids, has been somewhat of an embarrassment to the royal family. His father, Phillip, has continually bullied Charles to "toughen him

---

1. M. G. Warner, "Bush Battles the Wimp Factor," *Newsweek*, October 19, 1987, 28-31.
2. Guy D. Garcia, "Wimp No More," *Time*, April 24, 1989, 28-29.

up"—calling him a "wet" (British for "wimp") and taking sadistic measures that border on cruelty.[3]

Prince Charles has responded with a vengeance. He now plays a very spirited game of polo, flies aircraft at hair-raising velocities, and champions ambitious nationwide campaigns that benefit the poor and the environment.

What's so bad about being called a wimp? Let's begin by investigating the word's meaning. One dictionary says it's a slang term that means "a weak and ineffectual person." But its earliest known meaning extends back to 1909 at Cambridge University. Then it meant "a young, immature undergraduate girl."[4]

Some conjecture that "wimp" is a word that attempts to combine "wet" and "limp" in order to describe a person whose backbone is like spaghetti. Others say that it's somehow connected with the word "whimper," which is something a crybaby does.

For any world leader, creating an image of boldness is an absolute necessity. We might understand a leader's resentment at being called a wimp. But how about the rest of us? Are we likewise offended by anyone who tags us with this stigma?

Gentlemen, Take a Bow

On one hand, we laugh at wimpishness in leaders and even in our animals. I'm reminded of my mother-in-law's dog, who nearly had a nervous breakdown when a tiny mouse ran across the floor. Can you imagine what his reaction might have been at the sight of a burglar? Coco was a canine wimp.

But it's no laughing matter when *we're* the ones being accused of possessing this disreputable characteristic—especially if we're males. In fact, the term "wimp" is almost exclusively directed at us men. And this starts early in our lives.

Boys are allowed to be "marshmallows" but usually only up to a point. Unlike what they expect from our sisters, parents expect us to defend ourselves against playground bullies, do rigorous chores around the house, and perform like champions on soccer and football fields.

Granted, our female counterparts are more involved in sports than in times past, but there still exists a gender gap. In subtle ways, the ones made of "sugar and spice and everything nice" are cautioned about appearing excessively tomboyish.

3. Brad Darrach, "Prince Charles: A Dangerous Age," *People*, October 31, 1988, 97-101.
4. *New World Dictionary*, s.v. "wimp."

As children grow into the high school years, the same rigid expectations are apparent, though revealed in different ways.

Popular speaker and author Anthony Campolo delights in describing the jocks (athletes) at his inner-city high school in Philadelphia. They were so bad, says Tony, that it was necessary to have an obituary column in the school paper. These guys didn't walk down the halls like ordinary students; instead, they "moved." Their medal-laden letterman sweaters were so long that they almost dragged along the floor.

Then there were the wimps—whom everyone treated like pariahs. Talk about being conspicuous. It was impossible *not* to recognize them. They were the ones who wore galoshes (with pants tucked inside them) when it rained or carried their lunch in a brown paper bag—and *saved* the bag.

Campolo's high school was probably not all that different from the ones we attended. At my alma mater in Bell, California, we had the same well-defined camps of males: machos and wimps.

The former were popular, fulfilled, and in sync with the girls' dreams. The latter were ostracized by all—including themselves. They invariably ended up being consumed by nagging self-doubts, antisocial activities, and intense loneliness. Their options seemed restricted to joining the chess club, becoming a library hermit, or hanging out at the bowling alley.

So much for childhood and adolescence. Of course, males grow out of such a mentality as they enter adulthood. Right? Wrong.

*C*ircus elephants can be considered little more than two-ton wimps. As adults, all that's necessary to keep them stationary is a thin rope staked to the ground. They recall tugging and pulling against such a rope to escape when very young. At some point back then, they completely gave up—not temporarily, but for life. Even though they're now grown to gigantic proportions, it would be a small task to uproot the stake and be on their way. But their minds are heavily chained.

L. M. Boyd in the June 24, 1989, edition of the *Los Angeles Examiner* (page 2) wrote a column titled "Ostriches Find Thorns a Pain in the Face." He explained that in addition to burying their heads in the sand when they think danger is imminent, ostriches are spooked by the sight of anything thorny. They're "face shy"—fearful of a poke in the eye. Safari goers can drive alongside them at 50 miles per hour and wave a thorntree branch in their faces, and the birds will immediately slam on the brakes.

Second Verse, Same as the First

Certainly females are never completely exempt from criticism for being excessively wimpish. Avoiding challenges, being given to excessive pampering or cattiness, and constantly feigning helplessness invite some rebuke, especially from assertive members of their own sex.

But males who exhibit such behavior are more severely stigmatized. That's why we often react so vehemently at the slightest hint of accusation. Furthermore, many of us overcompensate in the opposite direction—become real he-men—to prove accusers wrong.

Question: What perpetuates this kind of thinking? Here are a few possible influences to consider:

1. *Macho media models are lauded in our culture.* From Paul Hogan to Clint Eastwood to Mel Gibson, the message comes out loud and clear: maleness and machismo are intertwined, or should be.

2. *Athletes capture our fondest admiration.* In perpetuating a "smash your opponent" image, jocks appear to be invincible. This is why baseball players sound gruff and never rub a bruise caused by a 98-mph fastball.

3. *Novelists and filmmakers have perpetuated an idealized image of the hardy Western cowboy,* whom Charles Swindoll describes as the "self-sufficient frontiersman—the squint-eyed, close-lipped, saddle-hardened, raw-boned fella who needs no one, trusts no one, and leans on no one (except maybe his horse)."[5]

4. *Some have (wrongly, I feel), interpreted the Bible to advocate a superman model.* In this model, authoritative men make women kowtow and children cringe. Intimidation is the order of the day. The child is not "spared"; nor, for that matter, is anyone else.

Some influences have pushed some of us into the arena of excess. As a result, some have become rather crude and insensitive—a cross between a bulldozer and a pit bull.

Then there are others of us who reject macho mania but who are likewise very uncomfortable with the opposite extreme: unisex. We feel that while men and women must be equally respected, they need not be alike. At this point, allow me to call an official time-out and reveal a wrinkle or two in my own psyche. Though it's no big deal with me, permit me to explain why I tend to see myself in this camp.

Time to Own Up

Now, please don't think I'm prepared to join a motorcycle gang, free-fall over the Grand Canyon, or rip off bandages if I confess to not wanting to be considered wimpishly effeminate.

5. Charles R. Swindoll, *Growing Deep in the Christian Life: Returning to Our Roots* (Minneapolis: Billy Graham Evangelistic Association, 1986), 349.

Given that admission, you might expect that I would shy away from certain behaviors that I (or others) might associate with that image. To be candid, some things I see men doing today seem about as manly as hosting a baby shower or shopping for doilies.

Here are some wimpish activities I find personally unappealing:

- *Wearing a diamond earring*—even if the person is a 300-pound tackle for the Chicago Bears.
- *Playing with a sponge football.* (This seems about as masculine as intercepting a powder puff.)
- *Having name monograms embroidered on shirtsleeve cuffs.*
- *Embracing pink as a favorite color.* (What brave nation ever went to battle waving a pink flag?)
- *Sporting fake macho attire.* (Clothes designer Danya Padilla once came up with the "sweat T-shirt" for those who hate exercise but want to look like a postworkout fitness enthusiast. It's faded gray with imprinted sweat marks.)

OK. So my preferences may seem a bit traditional. But why do I have this mild case of wimp-phobia? And why do so many of us guys—from world leaders to teenagers—share similar sentiments?

⁓

The color pink evidently has an emasculating effect. Traditionally, it has been reserved for such mild-mannered uses as little girls' rooms, bath soap, baby clothes, and bubble gum. But this is changing as a result of scientific color studies. It was found that the specific shade of Baker-Miller paint actually curbs aggression and seems to sap energy. Of the 153 subjects tested by Tacoma, Washington's Institute for Biosocial Research, all but two succumbed to the mood-inducing color, which affects the body's endocrine system and hormones, thereby slowing the heart.

Some prisons (for example, in San Jose, California) with pink walls have been able to reduce the number of guards.

—"Think Pink," *Campus Life*, January 1981, 30.

With a Capital C

Wimpishness connotes being sissified, spineless, comfort obsessed, passive, and overprotective. But more than anything else, it seems to imply a *lack of courage*.

Among all the nations of the world, courage counts big—with but a few scattered exceptions. Furthermore, it has assumed center stage throughout history. The ancient Egyptians gloried in their bravery, as did the Assyrians, Babylonians, Persians, Greeks, and Romans.

Today we stand in awe at the mention of Japanese kamikaze pilots, Afghan rebels, or China's heroic students at Tiananmen Square in Beijing.

Anthropologist G. Gorer
lists societies whose primary
goal is peaceful isolation
rather than conquest. These
include the Arapesh of New
Guinea, the Lepchas of Sikkim
in the Himalayas, and the Pyg-
mies of the Congo.

The social scientist notes
that these societies have the
following three things in common:

- Residing in inaccessible
  places, which other
  groups do not covet nor
  attempt to take from
  them.
- Orienting themselves primarily toward the simple,
  concrete pleasures of
  life—eating, drinking,
  sex—and when these are
  satisfied, so are they.
- Making few distinctions
  between males and fe-
  males (for example, no attempt is made to project
  an image of brave, aggres-
  sive masculinity).

—Lawrence S. Wrightsman, *Social
Psychology in the Seventies* (Belmont,
Calif.: Brooks/Cole Publishing Compa-
ny, 1972), 173-74.

Courage is a virtue not confined to any race, generation, or religion. It is ubiquitous and admired by all—even in one's enemies.

Author Charles Edward Jefferson states, "Three words . . . pierce the heart to the very center: one is 'thief,' the second is 'liar,' the third is 'coward.' [And] 'coward' is the most damning of them all."[6] If this is so, no word excites and motivates the human spirit more than "courage." Furthermore, no virtue is more needed today.

Samuel Johnson, renowned 18th-century English lexicographer, writer, and critic, put it succinctly: "Where courage is not, no other virtue can survive except by accident."[7]

The term "courage" is an integral part of our vocabulary. On a daily basis we seek en-*courage*ment, what someone has aptly called "courage transfusion." Ideas or people who help us face the world with boldness are greatly treasured. Conversely, we seek escape from *dis*couragement. Negativism and "downers" seem to suck all the oxygen from the air we breathe. They throw cold water on the coals of hope.

Unlike machismo, courage is a sterling quality of character that both men and women can equally aspire to. Little separates Joan of Arc from David Livingstone when it comes to manifesting this great virtue. It's as admirable in one gender as in another.

Likewise, authentic courage bursts the boundaries of age. I'll never forget a story featuring a young child with cancer, painfully but gallantly facing his imminent death.

Courage transcends time as well as space. It's no one nation's sole possession, nor does it belong to any particular age. Furthermore, it's a virtue

6. Charles Edward Jefferson, *The Character of Jesus* (New York: Grosset and Dunlap, 1908), 283-84.

7. C. S. Lewis, *Surprised by Joy* (New York: Harcourt, Brace and World, 1955), 161.

that's expandable to permeate vast civilizations and retractable to apply to isolated individuals. And whenever, wherever, and however it appears, people with it stand tall.

Nevertheless, courage is far more complex than what meets the eye—as is frequently so with life's greatest virtues. We must, therefore, venture far beyond the glib definitions and platitudes that the naive and less informed have disclosed. We must actively plumb the depths of its rich meanings with open minds and hearts. Then we'll see for ourselves why it's so esteemed by all people.

And we'll see why courage is absolutely essential for those of us who choose to follow the most courageous Man this world has ever known.

The ancient Romans purposely designed their soldiers' uniforms so that the backs were exposed and unprotected. Why? It would deter them from even considering retreat a viable option.

According to studies described by late pastor Earl Lee, five courageous, positive persons are required to merely cancel out the gloomy atmosphere created by one cowardly, negative individual. Implication: Most organizations cannot afford the luxury of having an inordinate number of cowardly, negative members.

2

A Tree, a Horse, and Plenty of Distance

Old age is not for cowards.
—Bette Davis

A coward dies a thousand deaths; the valiant dies but once.
—Julius Caesar

The worst human disaster can be met with courage
and gallantry when we meet it with God.
—William Barclay

Many of us have had to endure people who frequently brag about some famous ancestor. We're told that this person had unparalleled courage and, as a result, was always triumphant in spite of unbelievable odds. This bigger-than-life stalwart is reputed to have come on the nightmarish voyage of the *Mayflower*, single-handedly tamed the Western frontier, or annihilated some menacing Goliath.

Unfortunately, the Johnston lineage lacks such a folkloric hero by a long shot. No popes, martyrs, nobles, reformers, or celebrities are in our history. I've caught myself wishing that I were at least related to the owner of Johnston's Pie Company.

But before I evoke excessive sympathy, allow me to drop one family name. Help me decide whether this man qualifies as a famous ancestor. I recall his name always popping up at family reunions.

Joseph E. Johnston—ever heard of him? To say no is to reveal ignorance of United States Civil War history.

General Joe commanded a sizable portion of the Confederate Army. His battle record earned him Robert E. Lee's highest respect. So when it came time to repel the North's ruthless General Sherman at Atlanta, Johnston was moved from Chattanooga, Tennessee, to take command.

Well, that's about all I knew about the courageous battle fox until we visited Atlanta some time ago. We seized the opportunity to see the Cyclorama, a huge circular painting of that famous battle, the Battle of Atlanta. In this amazing work of art, the armies and terrain are vividly shown in three dimensions. And the account of the bloody battle is audibly presented.

Trying not to be too conspicuous, I squinted to see my famous relative. Finally the recorded voice pointed him out.

Are you ready for this? During the heat of the battle, old "blood-and-guts Joseph" was depicted as sitting leisurely on his horse under a shaded tree. Oh, yes—one more thing. The tree, horse, and Joseph were on the peak of a mountain that overlooked the city. You might say that he established a generous "safety zone" between himself and the battle.

From the start, Johnston had opposed fighting the battle—thinking that the carnage would serve no useful purpose. He had recommended a strategy of *retreating* to establish a better position.

When Stonewall Jackson heard of it, he was so angry that he saw to it that Johnston was relieved of his post. General John Bell Hood assumed command.

So much for ancestral bravery! When the real battle approached, Johnston was not around. His military cronies must have thought him to be little more than soggy milk toast. Or, in a phrase author Charles Swindoll likes to use, my forefather was perceived as a "yellow-livered mountain of Jell-O."

But that's him—and back then. What about us today? Do we frequently showcase unmistakable doses of raw courage?

It's All in a Day's Existence

According to some, those of us who get married, eat processed food, breathe polluted air—even get up in the morning—exhibit significant courage.

Situations that demand bold responses constantly present themselves. Do any of these sound familiar?

Courage is

- retrieving your wayward golf shot that has just shattered the window of an approaching car
- changing careers at 55, after being fired because your company tried to escape paying retirement
- proposing marriage to someone who has turned down three proposals in the last month
- sliding headfirst into home plate
- staying calm after the captain has just announced that the number two engine is on fire
- telling your spouse that you know he or she is having an affair

- going for marital counseling, even though you feel you're not at fault
- opening the envelope that contains your undisciplined child's report card
- agreeing to live with your mother-in-law
- going for a mammogram
- asking a hard-nosed boss for a raise
- initiating conversation with a stranger
- swimming in shark-infested waters to save someone
- signing the contract to purchase a home
- saying "No, thank you—I choose not to drink"
- shopping on the day before Christmas
- going on a diet
- refusing to fudge on your income tax forms
- venturing into the "combat zone" of a metropolitan-area freeway

Never would I discount the numerous courageous responses that we continuously make. But particular times especially stand out—times when we responded to great challenges in ways that surprised even ourselves.

The Scare of a Lifetime

The scene is Israel. The event is a recent Pepperdine University anthropological study tour that my wife and I conducted.

The students were rambunctious. One might even term them "daredevils." At a time when the Lebanese were continuously sending bombs into northern Israel (one blew out the side of the bus ahead of ours), these guys pleaded to cross the Lebanese border!

Some walked precariously close to fields in the desert that were filled with unexploded shells. Others leaned over the side of a deep cavern entrance in Jericho.

One day our bus driver, Schlomo, drove us to Masada, the high, flat-topped mountain that overlooks the Dead Sea. The fortress on top of the peak was built by Herod the Great and is notorious as the scene of the Jews' last stand against the Romans in A.D. 73.

Our guide, Money Ravid, was 30ish and wore a bright-colored orange beanie. He was

Masada looms bleak and ominous on the skyline. Rising steeply to 1,300 feet above the Dead Sea, it's topped by a broad plateau of 20 acres.

Here sat Herod's magnificent pleasure palace, with hanging gardens, a swimming pool, an elaborate bathhouse, vast stores, a synagogue, and ritual baths—all protected by sentry towers set at intervals along an encircling wall.

After the fall of Jerusalem in A.D. 70, a group of 960 Jewish zealots—men, women, and children—barricaded themselves on Masada and held it for three years. When conquest seemed imminent and the Romans were ready to burst in, Josephus tells us, the commander, Eleazar ben Yair, enjoined each defender to kill his family; then they "chose ten men by lot to slay all the rest … and when these ten had slain them all, they made the same rule for casting lots for themselves" (*Wars of the Jews*, book VII:9:1).

When the Romans eventually entered, they found amply stored food to show it was not lack of provisions that caused the Jews to surrender. Otherwise they found nothing but piles of corpses and a deathly silence.

Few experiences are more moving than being present at a ceremony on the summit of Masada, when the new recruits to the Parachute Division of Israel's Defense Army take their oath of allegiance to the state and solemnly swear that "Masada shall not fall again!"

—Sylvia Mann, *This Is Israel* (Herzlia, Israel: Palphot Ltd., 1980), 83-87.

a bit of a know-it-all. All the way to Masada he spoke of the glamorous site that awaited us, with its breathtaking view from the top.

We became more excited by the moment. The risk-loving students sported their climbing clothes; they intended to scale the heights. I assumed that our verbose guide would lead them.

But Money turned out to be a wimp. When the bus reached the foot of the mountain's treacherous cliffs, he announced that he would *not* be climbing. Instead, he would be riding the cable car to the top.

Well, he had me painted into a corner. I was not about to let my danger-loving students go alone. It was up to me to go with them. Reluctantly, I announced my intentions.

By now, you would think that our guide would have nothing more to say. Not so. He looked at me and declared, "Last week, I came here and climbed Masada with a fellow younger than you and in great condition. Halfway up he collapsed with a heart attack and died. The heat must have gotten to him."

His motormouth refused to stop. "Do you realize how easy it is to slip off the treacherous Snake Path when you're delirious with heat?"

Yes, I had some idea, and I realized that it would be well over 100 degrees that day.

I almost backed out then and there but knew that our gang would never let me forget it. I had to go through with this insane mission, leaving our Coke-sipping, smart-cracking, rested guide behind with my wife and a few of the girls.

We began the climb. At first it was a snap. The students joked, sang, and goofed off. But that was before the trail become alarmingly steep and much more narrow. Everyone became quiet as their faces reflected the tremendous strain and the torturous temperature.

The girl behind me suddenly slipped on some loose gravel. But she miraculously managed to stop herself at the cliff's edge. She muttered to herself, "Well, you almost ate the big one." Although it was college student jargon, I didn't have to ask what she meant.

As I was helping her recover, someone pointed upward and yelled. It was Money, my wife, and the girls going overhead in the cable car, yelling out some taunting remarks. For them the ride was no more frightening than a visit to Disneyland.

We kept trudging along. Slipping. Sliding. Straining. When I began to feel more confident about our chances of making it, one of the heartiest members of the group suddenly stopped and clutched a large boulder. He was obviously hyperventilating and was perhaps even in the throes of a heatstroke. We stopped to provide some shade and liquid. He finally responded, and we started climbing once again. A short distance ahead, the young man was stricken again. This went on for the remainder of the way.

Several other students were looking very peaked and dizzy. More were slipping now, and some were scaring themselves by looking down. The view from the frighteningly high trail gave me the sensation of being on the tip of the wing of an airplane in flight.

At last the end came. We had made it to the top—and with no casualties. Those awaiting us at the summit let out a cheer and rushed to us with refreshing drinks. Money just shook his head, sighed, and looked the other way. But we didn't care. We had made it—in spite of our fears, the heat, the steepness, and all the other dangers. We proudly walked over together to a vendor and bought T-shirts boasting, "I climbed Masada."

To some who have endured far more, our feat might seem very insignificant; but to us it seemed like a very courageous adventure. In my case, it was an adventure forced upon me, but it was an adventure nevertheless.

We had experienced firsthand the tremendous exhilaration that accompanies beating the odds, challenging the difficult, surmounting the fears—and claiming the victory.

Did we manifest authentic courage? It sure felt like it. But was it really? Let's focus on the intricate meanings associated with this honored virtue. To do so might encourage all of us to climb many "Masadas" in our future lives.

A Quality That Distinguishes

The Random House Dictionary defines courage as "the ability to face difficulty or danger with firmness and without fear."[1]

---

1. *The Random House Dictionary*, s.v. "courage."

Allow me to edit that definition to read "the ability and commitment to *endure and challenge* difficulty or danger with firmness *in spite of* fear."

For purposes of clarification, let's contrast courage with some other concepts that are often confused with it.

First, courage is not the same as "impulsive reaction." The latter is a knee-jerk response that occurs without serious reflection or reference to moral principles. Usually it consists of rapid retaliation for perceived threat.

To fly off the handle in a fit of rage is neither commendable nor courageous. It betrays a basic weakness of character. Honk at slow drivers. Yell at an unfair boss. Slap a disobedient child. Cuss out a waitress who spills hot coffee on your new suit. Some may see these behaviors as courageous. Don't believe them for a minute. These actions reveal a real problem. An ocean of distance exists between such infantile reactions and the real thing.

Second, courage is certainly not synonymous with "indifference to fear, pain, or stress." The most courageous persons are those who have hearts that pound like muffled drums and fears that soar, yet they still walk resolutely into the jaws of trial and danger. For them, courage is a purposive and conscious choice rather than an attempt to deny reality.

My experience as a marriage counselor attests to the fact that most divorces occur because one or both partners attempt to block out fear, pain, or stress. They engage in continual denial, gingerly sidestepping their problems. As a result, their psychic "gunnysacks" begin to fill—and finally break.

How much better it would be to air grievances, to admit pain, to talk over fears! Granted, that requires true courage, especially when it involves close intimates.

Courage is light-years away from denial. Rather, it suggests the opposite.

Finally, courage is not necessarily synonymous with heroic action. For one thing, the former involves more being than doing. Here the focus is on inner character: values, priorities, mind-set, attitudes, commitments.

To be open to new ways of thinking requires courage, as does developing personal maturity and sensitivity. For many, achieving self-honesty is more difficult than fighting in wars.

Certainly, courage will involve action. Once we develop an inner boldness, based on conviction rather than expediency, we will take courageous action—action that sets us off from the crowd and makes us independent of its approval, action that's in harmony with the inner selves we have created.

Will such action be perceived as "heroic"? Not usually.

Recently a lady ran her car into a lake behind our house. A young man who witnessed the whole thing tore off his shoes and dived in. After a great struggle, he freed the lady and brought her to the surface. His response to a reporter is typical of a courageous person. When asked, "Do you see yourself as a hero?" he replied, "Not in the least. I simply responded the way any responsible person should have."

If we're courageous, we'll constantly be involved in similar—but far less dramatic—actions: returning lost money, telling it straight to an alcoholic friend, voting our conscience, standing with a powerless person who has been wronged by another.

On second thought, perhaps some of these *do* border on the heroic!

Refuse to Be Tricked

As we've seen, courage must be separated from facsimiles and counterfeits. This is the first step in gaining a full appreciation of and desire for the real thing. As long as we buy into a caricature of this essential quality, we'll fail to absorb it into our lives.

Once again, courage does not mean impulsively, instantly avenging every wrong or correcting every inaccuracy. Often the most courageous action is to patiently wait for the right time and opportunity.

Likewise, fear, pain, and stress are about as likely to disappear as California earthquakes, Kansas tornadoes, and Texas flash floods—and with as little warning. They're trials that everyone must bear.

But make no mistake about it: the courageous person is better able to cope. Why? Because he or she is able to change fear, pain, and stress from liabilities and depressors into assets and motivators.

As for heroics, we must realize that most courage issues forth in quiet, unnoticed, and unappreciated ways: no brass bands, no newspaper accolades, no medals of honor—just the inner satisfaction that comes with realizing that courage is its own reward. It does wonders for ourselves and for anyone else who chooses to notice.

Former United States President Abraham Lincoln said, "My purpose in living is to plant a flower where a weed once grew." If enough of us plant flowers of courage, our world will be a much better place.

There is more to understand about this marvelous virtue. Once we distinguish it from its counterfeits, we must explore its many forms. Let's see how many of these we possess and which of them are closely related to Christian discipleship.

3

A Lot like Ice Cream

It is not that I'm afraid to die—I just don't want
to be there when it happens.
—Woody Allen

I cannot praise a fugitive and cloistered virtue, unexercised
and unbreathed, that never sallies out and sees her adversity,
but slinks out of the race where that immortal garland is to be run for, not without
dust and heat.
—John Milton

If you stop and ask yourself why you are not so devoted as
the [early] Christians, your own heart will tell you that it is
neither through ignorance nor inability, but purely because
you never thoroughly intended it.
—William Law

There are as many kinds of courage as there are flavors of ice cream. And, like that favorite dessert, they all seem to be extremely appealing.

We've heard numerous synonyms for courage. Among them are backbone, grit, mettle, heart, spunk, and daring. Likewise, clichés related to the virtue are seemingly endless: "Run the gauntlet." "Bell the cat." "Take the bull by the horns." "Take heart." "Keep your chin up." "Keep a stiff upper lip." "Stand the gaff." "Stick to your guns."

Though similar in meaning, these references to boldness highlight a rich panorama of different perspectives. We are well advised to scrutinize the various shades of meaning in order to fully comprehend this universally revered virtue.

Though classifications are quite arbitrary, for the sake of clarification let us state that courage seems to exist in five basic forms. We will briefly explore each of them.

1. Fortitude

Obviously, in all of us the physical (kinetic) is closely interrelated with the mental (cognitive) and emotional (cathectic). Nevertheless, there exists a brand of courage that's calculated to cause extreme discomfort to our bodies. Some call it "moxie." I call it "fortitude."

To bite the bullet and take punishing licks is a form of courage that's especially associated with athletes.

Ready for a baseball trivia question? Who is Clint Courtney? If you're unsure, don't bother requesting the answer from Cooperstown, New York. Clint never came close to making it into the Baseball Hall of Fame.

This guy was not a legend in his own time—not even in his own mind. He was primarily a memory maker for his family and a few die-hard fans who were inspired by his tremendous fortitude.

Clint played catcher for the Baltimore Orioles in the 1950s. During his career he earned the nickname of Scrap Iron, implying that he was hard, weathered, tough.

Old Scrap broke no records—only bones. He had little power or speed on the base paths. As for grace and style, he made the easiest play look rather difficult. But armed with mitt and mask, Scrap Iron never flinched from any challenge. Batters often missed the ball and caught his shin. Their foul tips nipped his elbow. Runners fiercely plowed into him, spikes first, as he defended home plate.

Though often doubled over in agony, and flattened in a heap of dust, Clint Courtney never quit. Invariably, he would slowly get up, shake off the dust, punch the pocket of his mitt once, twice, and nod to his pitcher to throw another one.

The game would go on and Courtney with it, scarred, bruised, clutching his arm in pain, but determined to continue. He resembled a prisoner of war, with tape, splints, braces, and other kinds of paraphernalia that wounded people wear. Some made fun of him, calling him insane, a masochist. Others remember him as a true champion.

Like many of the other kinds of courage, this type can be carried to the extreme. But Scrap Iron's approach to baseball should be our approach to life's game. We are thrown many curveballs, we take our blows, and we endure plenty of unexpected losses.[1] But when the dust clears, we must somehow stagger to our feet and invite life's next pitch.

---

1. Diane Cole, "Old Scrap Iron," *Psychology Today*, May 1988, 66 ff.

2. Bravery

Although it may overlap into several of the other areas, the kind of courage that responds to a crisis is termed "bravery." And it's best understood by focusing on a real-life drama.

A heavy, swirling snowstorm had choked Washington, D.C.'s streets on a frigid January morning in 1982. Fourteenth Street Bridge, spanning the Potomac River, resembled a parking lot. Suddenly a blue, green, and white jetliner broke out of the opaque sky, losing altitude and heading straight for the crowded bridge.

Motorists gasped in horror as the doomed aircraft raked the surface of the northbound span, sheared the tops off several cars, then plunged into the icy waters as it broke apart.

Air Florida's flight 90, a Boeing 737 bound for Tampa, had crashed with over 80 people aboard. Only 5 would survive.

Though unreachable, victims were still visible under rescue workers' lights. Trapped in their seat belts in the split and sunken fuselage, they were slowly covered by the river's ice.

Paramedic Gene Windsor maneuvered his helicopter dangerously close to the water's surface as he towed the few survivors to shore with a lifeline. The craft's skids could easily have iced, which would have caused him to lose control.

Two psychologists, Darley and Latane, studied the conditions under which people are or are not willing to help others in an emergency. In essence, they concluded that responsibility is diffused.

The more people who are present in an emergency situation, the less likely it is that any one of them will offer help. This is popularly called "the bystander effect."

In the actual experiment, when one bystander was present, 85 percent offered help. When two were present, 62 percent offered help. When five were present, only 31 percent offered help.

—Lawrence S. Wrightsman, *Social Psychology in the Seventies* (Monterey, Calif.: Brooks/Cole Publishing Company, 1972), 33-34.

Truly, Windsor's bravery was exemplary. But there were others like him.

One woman, 22-year-old Priscilla Tirado, lost her grip on the rope and was on the verge of drowning. An onlooker, Lenny Skutnik, suddenly plunged in and, risking his life, saved her. A medical exam revealed that Priscilla's body temperature was so low that she was only a few minutes away from cardiac arrest.

But there was another person, Arland D. Williams, whose bravery was especially heartwarming. He was among the six who clung to the aircraft's tail, waiting for the helicopter to pull them to shore. According to witness-es, Mr. Williams repeatedly passed the lifeline to the others rather than grabbing onto it himself.

When the chopper finally returned for him, he had slipped beneath the surface. With reverence, Windsor later said, "I've never seen one man with that much commitment."[2]

What sharp contrast to a scene that occurred on a New York street nearly two decades before! Kitty Genovese was slowly and brutally stabbed to death. At least 38 of her neighbors witnessed the attack and heard her screams. In the course of a 90-minute episode, her attacker was actually frightened away but then returned to finish her off. Yet not once during that period did any neighbor assist her or even telephone the police.

The bravery displayed in the Washington event makes us rejoice in our humanity. We stand tall. But the scenario in New York, with its vivid display of cowardice, causes us to feel sorrow and shame.

Certainly bravery is a kind of courage we need to see frequently. It's essential for our nation, for our communities, and for our homes.

3. Valor

When courage is transferred to the battlefield, it's referred to as valor. Though similar in many respects to the kinds of courage already discussed, valor is motivated by the added dimensions of intense patriotism, accentu-ated morale, extreme conformity, and a great feeling of teamwork—even with those at home.

One more thing: soldiers infused with valor tend to be very optimistic about their chances for victory. In a speech to Pepperdine University stu-dents, Los Angeles Dodger manager Tommy Lasorda declared that George Custer had to be the greatest optimist who ever lived.

Why? Before charging into the Battle of the Little Bighorn, he yelled these words to his soldiers: "Don't take any prisoners!" Now that's real opti-mism!

As a boy in Hattiesburg, Mississippi, I vividly recall the return of a wartime hero, Henry A. Commisky. With thousands of other people and brass bands, I greeted the white-uniformed, smiling hero. Every kid in the city jammed into the community center to hear the words of this Korean War hero.

He began by telling us what he had done. His entire unit had been ambushed by soldiers with machine guns. In the hail of bullets, he rushed

---

2. "Death on the Potomac," *Newsweek*, January 25, 1982, 26.

to overtake one of the mounted weapons, wheeled it around, and subdued scores of Communist soldiers. He saved his unit and even forced the enemy to retreat.

Our town gave Henry and his bride a new house. It seemed a small reward for his valor.

Nice story. Great ending. But, to be candid, valor can get out of hand. Who hasn't grimaced at the gory details of the My Lai incident—when Lieutenant Calley and his regiment killed and mutilated scores of innocent Vietnamese citizens? It was a clear case of what social psychologists often term "overobedience."

Perhaps every virtue, including valorous courage, when pushed to its extreme, becomes a vice. If so, Christian military personnel must be on guard.

With good reason, we turn to the next kind of courage to offer such a balance—a balance that emerges from an enlightened and sensitive conscience.

4. Resoluteness

Resoluteness is the type of courage based on inner conviction. It springs forth from a deep commitment to some moral principle. As a result, a resolution is made to tenaciously fight (or endure) for that belief.

Here again the distinction is a matter of focus. The spotlight is on a strongly held value. And all, even one's entire life, is subordinated to the latter. Perhaps Martin Luther King Jr. was referring to resoluteness when he wrote, "A person is not prepared to live unless there is a cause for which he is ready to die."

King pointed to a shining example of this virtue. He once described this woman as "the great fuse that led to the modern stride toward freedom." But actually she made that stride while sitting still. Let me relate her inspiring story.

This woman possesses no aura of distinction. There's no commanding uniqueness about her manner and dress. Yet her story is one of the most inspirational to emerge from the Civil Rights Movement of the United States.

On the evening of December 1, 1955, Rosa Parks caught the Cleveland Avenue bus in Montgomery, Alabama, to return home from her job as a seamstress. She knew the ride would take 15 minutes, so she leaned back to relax.

Soon the bus filled to capacity. The white bus driver noticed that this Black woman was occupying a seat in the "white section"—while a white passenger was standing. Yelling out, he ordered the offender to the rear.

Now Rosa wasn't one to whimsically defy authority. She was no rabble-rousing integrationist—just a simple, 42-year-old garment worker who wanted to rest after a hard day's labor.

But in Rosa's mind the bus driver had violated a basic moral principle. Granted, he had the law behind him, but it still didn't seem right. So she remained seated.

In so doing, Rosa did not make a scene—no screams, no whines, no threats. She simply refused to move, thus making it necessary for those who wanted to force her to get up to make the next move.

The frightened Black lady was arrested, jailed, and brought to trial. A 26-year-old minister, Martin Luther King Jr., heard about the case and on December 5 urged Montgomery's Blacks to boycott the bus system. They did.

How did the episode end? Buses were desegregated the following year, and the era of passive resistance began that culminated in the signing of the Civil Rights Act of the 1960s.

Mrs. Parks paid dearly for her courage. Her husband, a barber, became ill from the stress. The family was forced to move to Detroit. Mrs. Parks had to do sewing and alterations at home.

Today Rosa Parks is greatly revered. What was the inner resolution she had and resolutely defended? Very simply, she strongly believed that human dignity cannot interminably be undermined by brute force. And it was not.[3]

The Upward Spiral

The foregoing courage types overlap and are certainly not an exhaustive list. Yet they seem to be among the most noteworthy and frequently evidenced aspects of courage in our world.

Each mentioned is commendable in its own right. Nevertheless, in my thinking, the order in which they're presented suggests the ascending order of their value—from fortitude to resoluteness. But most of us are grateful for courage, however, whenever, and wherever it has existed. Sure, some forms of courage have been badly misdirected, but most have been of great benefit to humanity.

Like Charles Swindoll, I'm glad that some very special persons refused to take the easy way, to listen to the advice of quitters, pessimists, doomsayers, and wet blankets.

---

3. *The Negro Almanac: A Reference Work on the Afro-American*, ed. Harry A Ploski and James Williams (New York: John Wiley and Sons, 1983), 31, 228, 1325-26.

I'm glad, for example,

- that *Thomas Edison* did not give up on the lightbulb, even though his helpers seriously doubted the thing would ever work
- that *Martin Luther* refused to back down when the church doubled her fists and clenched her teeth
- that *Michelangelo* kept pounding and painting, regardless of the pope's put-downs
- that *Charles Lindbergh* decided to fly over the ocean when everyone else said it was ridiculous and dangerous
- that *Corrie ten Boom's* father said yes to frightened Jews who needed a hiding place
- that Julliard School of Music saw past leg braces and a wheelchair to admit an unlikely violin student named *Perlman*[4]

We could add to this list. Some of us might deserve to be on the list ourselves. But it's crucial that we not stop, nor even linger, in our quest for courage.

We need to examine one more type of courage. Without a doubt, it's far superior to any types we've mentioned—and often includes them. Furthermore, we need not awkwardly grope for this prize. There is One who has led the way and desires to lead *our* way. His name is Jesus. In a real way, it seems as if He invented courage—having relinquished heaven to face such opposition on earth.

Let's closely examine this final form of courage by going to the Source. For it's in His character that this form is best revealed.

To do so will be to draw strength, receive guidance, and commit ourselves to the special type of courage that made Him so triumphant. For it's the same kind that distinguishes us as His followers.

---

4. Charles R. Swindoll, *The Quest for Character* (Portland, Oreg.: Multnomah Press, 1967), 134-35. Copyright © 1982 by Charles R. Swindoll, Inc. Used by permission of Zondervan Publishing House.

Part 2

COURAGE—
WHY IS IT SO ESSENTIAL FOR CHRISTIANS?

4

O Holy Knight

A popular writer declares, "Our Lord Jesus held nothing back when He left heaven, lived on earth, and went for it—all the way to the Cross—and beyond."[1]

Did Christ have courage? Do lions roar? Is Alaska cold in winter? He wrote the book on courage, and it contains all four forms we've examined.

Fortitude. How else can we explain His serenity in the boat with panic-stricken disciples during the tumultuous storm (Luke 8:22-25)?

Bravery. The number of crises He faced resembles airplanes backed up in holding patterns over Chicago. They arrive one after another and often simultaneously.

He lovingly intervened for the demon-possessed (Mark 5:1-20), the lepers (Luke 5:12-14), the hungry (John 6:5-14), the deaf (Mark 7:31-35), and even the dead (Luke 8:49-56).

Valor. Granted, our Lord was not a soldier. But He waged continuous war against assaulting armies: the scribes and Pharisees (Mark 7:1-16, KJV); money changers in the Temple, along with the wicked chief priests who supported them (11:15-18); and even a lynch mob (Luke 4:16-30).

Resoluteness. Our Savior clearly articulated support for righteous, though unpopular, principles. His Sermon on the Mount was revolutionary—cutting cross-grain against this world's value system (Matt. 5—7). An-

---

1. Swindoll, *Quest for Character*, 135. Copyright © 1982 by Charles R. Swindoll, Inc. Used by permission of Zondervan Publishing House.

other time, when He healed on the Sabbath and declared His equality with His Father, the Jews threatened His life (John 5:1-18).

A biting rebuke of lawyers issued forth from His lips: "Woe to you, because you load people down with burdens they can hardly carry, and you yourselves will not lift one finger to help them" (Luke 11:46).

Nor were His disciples spared. He chastised them for rebuking little children (Matt. 19:13-14), not having enough faith to cast out demons (Mark 9:18-19), and conspiring to obtain positions of power (Matt. 20:20-28).

Jesus possessed all of these forms of courage: fortitude, bravery, valor, and resoluteness. In addition, He manifested a fifth quality of courage that transcends even these four. For lack of a better term, I'll refer to this quality as "chivalry."

One dictionary defines chivalry as "the qualities expected of a knight, as courage, generosity, and courtesy . . . gallant[ry] to[ward] women."[2]

Let's see how Jesus is our "holy Knight."

Chivalry

Add heroism to the four kinds of courage discussed in the last chapter. Then combine heroism with gallantry, courtesy, and a gentle graciousness toward the weak and helpless. The whole package suggests "chivalry"—a word originating from the days of medieval knighthood.

The imagery is refreshing to ponder. We visualize troops of brave men carrying brightly colored banners, riding forth to protect the weak, maintain righteousness, and uphold justice.

Women were special objects of the knights' care. By defending women and all who were at the mercy of the brute powers of a barbaric world, knights won for themselves a shining place in history. And they gave chivalry a splendor that will never fade.

Jesus of Nazareth embodied the best of knightly virtues. He journeyed forth "clad in armor of a peerless manhood" to shield the defenseless, promote the holy, and reveal a sacrificial life that would inspire the world. He stands forever as the Knight of knights.[3]

In what specific ways was our Lord chivalrous? Let us look at five scenes, as though they were color slides that reveal some idea of the depths of His fathomless courage.

---

2. *Random House Dictionary*, s.v. "chivalry."
3. Jefferson, *Character of Jesus*, 171-85.

Water Shared by Brothers

Scene number one: the Jordan River. There appeared to be little reason for Jesus to take part in the ritual of baptism. His heart was unstained by sin, and John's baptism was one of repentance.

Furthermore, His participation might lead to misunderstanding. How would the opened sky, the dove, and the voice from heaven be interpreted by those present? Indeed, there were great risks involved. John even did his best to dissuade Jesus.

But Jesus went through with it. Why? Because He desired to intimately identify with His sinful countrymen—to climb down into the trenches with them and share their experiences firsthand.

Though sinless, Jesus began His ministry by linking himself with those who endured the burden of transgression and cried out for deliverance (Mark 1:1-11). And that began a pattern that lasted until the end of His earthly sojourn. Unlike many Christians today, He was never satisfied with keeping sinners at arm's length. Instead, His arms embraced them tightly.

Why? Let's hear His answer to some Pharisees. They had heard how Jesus dined with Matthew—a man of questionable character at the time. So they asked His disciples, "Why does your teacher eat with tax collectors and 'sinners'?"

Overhearing the question, He answered, "It is not the healthy who need a doctor, but the sick. . . . I have not come to call the righteous, but sinners" (Matt. 9:11-13).

Jesus expects us to come out from behind cloistering church walls. Linkage must be made. Significant identification must be established between those of us who are spiritually healthy and have access to the Doctor's medicine (His Word and presence), and those who are mired in sin.

Palestine's Mayo Clinic

Suffering and physical distress pierced our Lord's heart. And He was well aware of His nation's neglect of the sick.

Jesus' world knew no Medicare, no health insurance, no hospitals. Sure—the wealthy could hire trained personnel to alleviate pain and lessen the terrors associated with dying. But the poor suffered unattended and died unrelieved.

The mentally disturbed received no proper care. On the contrary, people considered them demon-possessed and drove them from town. The tragic result was that they were forced to live in desolate, uninhabited places—such as deserts and cemeteries. Their troubled cries and loud shrieks terrorized persons passing by.

Jesus pitied the dispossessed. But even more important, He dared to reach out in love. Mark 5 vividly illustrates this conclusion.

Scene number two: a small fishing boat, with Jesus inside, makes its way across the Sea of Galilee to the region of the Gerasenes. A greatly disturbed tomb dweller with superhuman strength rushes out to meet Him.

Neither chains nor irons could bind this man—nor did anyone attempt to stifle his blood-curdling cries or restrain his self-inflicted mutilations made with sharp rocks. He was a ghastly sight, and he frightened all—except Jesus.

Worst of all, the disheveled man was so saturated with evil spirits that they became his ventriloquist. He himself remained silent while they spoke through his mouth and pleaded for mercy, knowing of Christ's power to destroy them.

In May 1987 I visited the northeastern side of the Sea of Galilee, the place thought to be the exact site of Jesus' casting out of the demons into a swineherd. My student Bo Cassell and I climbed the mountain to visualize how the event might have occurred.

There are open fields where the pigs might have been kept. At the western side of the fields were cliffs overlooking the water. Evidently these were the very cliffs from which the pigs hurled themselves. The ruins of an ancient church were just below us, marking the site and commemorating the miracle.

Jesus expelled the demons into a herd of swine, which plunged off cliffs into the lake—much to the consternation of their owners.

Then we see another picture. There stands a dressed, composed, rational human being. So radically changed was the grave dweller that those who had known him before were absolutely petrified of the man—and also of our omnipotent Savior (v. 15).

By the time persons with twisted perspectives had disseminated the story, the entire region was in pandemonium. As a result, the people pled with the Great Physician to leave their region (v. 17).

Who would ever think that offering relief to a pitiful man would result in rejection? Jesus knew beforehand what their reaction would be, but that didn't stop Him. He went straight ahead and followed His agenda of love. That took courage—lots of it.

Jesus had no regrets about delivering the man. Forgive my "loose cannon conjecture," but as the Lord's boat slid off the sand onto the lake, I can imagine Him smiling and saying to himself, "It's too bad about all those pigs, but those Gentiles shouldn't be eating all that bacon anyway."

Strictly Generic; Definitely Not Designer!

Between Galilee and Judea lived the Samaritans, half-Jewish and half-pagan people who had morally degenerated from the high ideals of earlier days. Jews referred to them as apostates and treated them like lepers.

Rarely would a true Hebrew journey through that defiled land. *Scene number three*, however, reveals the Good Shepherd not only passing through but also lingering to minister to His sheep—just as He did with the Judeans and Galileans.

No man could intimately socialize with Samaritans without paying a great price. Jesus paid it. People gnashed their teeth and hissed, "You are a Samaritan" (John 8:48). In their minds, this was the most derogatory thing they could possibly say, but it didn't cause Christ to lose heart or to be diverted from His mission.

He healed Samaritans and pointed them to God. Though the rabbis considered them to be outcasts and banned them from Temple ceremonies, Jesus warmly took them in.

In fact, when He offered a parable that depicted His model for true righteousness, its star was a Samaritan. Not incidentally, the villains were portrayed by Jewish ecclesiastical bureaucrats (Luke 10:30-37). One of the most chivalrous things anyone can ever do is to confront entrenched prejudice. People who champion the cause of the attacked are frequently made targets of abuse. But the Knight of Galilee unflinchingly pursued His course. His heavenly marching orders included taking a stand for these abandoned, hopeless people. And He obeyed—which was His style.

Woman: Animal, Vegetable, or Mineral?

As with all true knights, it's in His treatment of women that Christ's chivalry reaches a very lofty expression.

In His part of the world, females were not treated fairly. They were never perceived as being equal to men.

Jesus boldly defended the women of His day. He attacked divorce laws, which put women at the mercy of men. Husbands could abandon their wives simply by signing a statement of declaration.

This was an open-eyed, defiant misrepresentation of Moses' Law. Jesus knew it. They knew it. Jesus knew that they knew it, and it made them angry. Our Lord proclaimed the principle of "indissolubility" in relationship to marriage; marriage is for life, period (Matt. 5:27-32).

In those days adulterous men went about scot-free. Not so with women. Those caught were stoned. One such woman was dragged to Jesus in an attempt to entrap Him. Would He obey Mosaic Law and advise that she be destroyed, or would He declare another of His "heresies"?

They received their answer that day—an extremely courageous answer that pointed a finger at the accusers. Result: a forgiven and very relieved woman went her way—and some embarrassed men stormed away with guilt and anger (John 8:3-11).

Scene number four: Jacob's well. This is the place where Jesus offers the ultimate example of His respect for womanhood. It was here that He was nonkosher in three ways. He spoke to a woman in public. She was a "despicable" Samaritan. To compound His "crime" even further, she happened to be an overachiever when it came to blatant fornication. Talk about questionable credentials—a good Jew certainly would not give her the time of day, much less carry on a conversation with her.

But Jesus gave her much more than that; He offered her eternal life. He did it without condescending or insulting. And why not? It's exactly what we would expect this holy Knight to do.

It can safely be said that no person who has walked this earth did more for women than our Lord. He treated them like real people—not toys, animals, or even like subordinate humans. Christ regarded women as bona fide, genuinely equal human beings.

As impressive as Christ's treatment of women is, I hasten to reveal *scene number five.* In many ways, it demonstrates His chivalry more than any other instance. It occurs somewhere at the base of Mount Hermon in northern Palestine—perhaps near Caesarea Philippi.

The Galvanized Gaze

To speak up for a noble cause is commendable. To offer a compassionate heart and a helping hand to the helpless is admirable. But the highest expression of chivalry is offering to die for others. John's Gospel states, "Greater love has no one than this, that he lay down his life for his friends" (15:13).

Jesus was neither a sick masochist nor a dreamer of posthumous headlines of grandeur. He was not even caught up in the kind of battle psychology that causes people to throw themselves into enemy fire. Rather, He calmly, clear-mindedly, and compassionately chose to give His life for the greatest cause ever—eternal life.

Capture the setting in Luke 9. The Lord had just come from His glorious transfiguration on Mount Hermon (vv. 28-36). Peter, James, and John were there to witness His translucent face and clothes. They also saw Moses and Elijah—the greatest lawgiver and the greatest prophet—appear before them.

Why did these saints make an appearance? To talk about His soon approaching death (v. 31), and primarily to offer encouragement to the Lamb, who would shortly be slain for many. In essence, it was a "Come on—You can do it!" pep talk.

Well, down the mountain came Jesus and the three disciples—only to be met by a convulsing, demon-possessed child whom the other disciples had been unable to help. Exasperated, Jesus called them an "unbelieving and perverse generation" (v. 41). Then He healed the lad.

While the crowd marveled, the Lord turned to the disciples and said, "Listen carefully to what I am about to tell you: The Son of Man is going to be betrayed into the hands of men" (v. 44). Unfortunately He received no sympathy nor even understanding. "They did not grasp it, and they were afraid to ask him about it" (v. 45).

It was as if they were saying, "Look—don't dump this depressing thought on us now. Besides, what You're talking about is over our heads." As the familiar saying goes, there is none so blind as the one who *will not* see.

These same disciples begin arguing over which of them was the great-est. Jesus slowly reached out to grasp the hand of a child and snuggled him to His breast, saying, "He who is least among you all—he is the greatest" (v. 48). Case closed—almost.

John began to tattle on someone, a man who had successfully driven out demons in the Master's name. His big sin? "He is not one of us" (v. 49). This man was a believer, no doubt, but not one of the pedigreed—not one of the 12 "biggies." Kindly but firmly, Jesus offered John a lesson on toler-ance.

The Transfiguration had been awesome. Though the subject dis-cussed was His death, the Transfiguration provided a real uplift. And yet we see these stark examples of sin and immaturity in the lives of the ones He had gently taught for so long.

Must He die for these and their faithless generation? Absolutely—for every last one of them, from the most righteous and obedient follower to the most heinous criminal.

Verse 51 is cryptic in its imagery: "Jesus resolutely set out for Jerusa-lem." He faced the music. He gazed at the tragedy that lay before Him and intentionally took the first step toward that destination.

In so doing, He agreed to endure the events that are now so familiar to us: betrayals, scourging, jeers, false accusations, pain too intense to imag-ine. He looked ahead and saw it all in vivid, excruciating detail.

But His face remained set in that direction. He was not looking back like Lot's wife (Gen. 19:17, 23-26; Luke 17:28-33), not second-guessing like Elijah under the juniper (broom) tree (1 Kings 19:3-8), and not attempting to maneuver or sidestep. He did not plead "special case status" like those who disdain military conquest; He did not delay.

No, our Lord set His face resolutely toward Jerusalem. Though He reached out for added strength and confirmation in the Garden of Gethsemane, He never cowered or flinched a muscle until He reached the Cross. Picture Him as He courageously marches onward: "trampling on all the precious things on earth, putting under His feet the ambitions by which the hearts of other men are fired, trampling into the dust the prizes and the joys of life . . . Jesus placed every one of them beneath His feet."[4]

A Knight of His God's Heavenly Order

Jesus Christ was chivalrous, like the loyal, courageous, and compassionate knights of many centuries ago. He shared so many of their graces and virtues. He had nerve, mettle, and the intrepidity of the bravest of knights, together with a winsome and divine graciousness history can't match.

Yet it's important to remember that Jesus Christ was the holy Knight of God's heavenly order—which distinguishes Him from medieval warriors in important ways:

- They primarily sought adventure; His adventure came to Him.
- They clad themselves in metal; His only protection was the white innocence of an unspoiled heart.
- They possessed the skills of soldiers; His skills were those of a physician.
- They fought to lay their enemies in the dust; His prowess was that of a friend and brother.
- They delighted in pomp and glory; though not in the least bit timid, He shied away from the spotlight of publicity.
- They were ostentatious in style and manner; He went about doing good inconspicuously.
- They protected the distressed and upheld the right but often failed to live stainless lives; He, the Prince of knights and Kings of all hosts of chivalry, conquered—but lived His life without even the smallest trace of sin.[5]

High but Not out of Reach

When hearing any of my Lord's virtues extolled, I've often asked myself, "How can I ever hope to reach His example?" Rousseau was right

---

4. Ibid., 292-93.
5. Ibid., 183-84.

when he wrote, "If the life and death of Socrates were those of a sage, the life and death of Jesus are those of . . . God."[6]

In a real way my feelings are justified. The creature can forget about approximating the Creator—especially when it comes to having His boldness. Yet I also realize that resting my case here is a cop-out, one that uncounted numbers have utilized to sidestep His expectations.

Because God lives in my heart, I do have power—Son-power. I can be bold in faith as I affirm His presence and tackle challenges that He brings to my attention. I can do this without feeling the least bit arrogant.

Just *how* does this occur, according to God's Word? And who are some mortals, like us, who have utilized His power supply to manifest His kind of courage? Our next chapter begins by addressing these questions.

---

6. Ibid., 294.

5

$\mathcal{T}$HE $\mathcal{S}$IGNIFICANT $\mathcal{I}$NSIGNIFICANT

Even if you're on the right track, you'll get run over if you just sit there.
—Will Rogers

Moral courage almost never appears
except as part of that greater entity called character.
—Allan Nevins

Jesus came not to make life easy, but to make men great.
—William Barclay

Who was United States Senator Edmund G. Ross of Kansas? I suppose you could call him a Mr. Nobody. No law bears his name. Not a single list of Senate greats mentions his service.

Yet when Ross entered the Senate in 1866, he was considered the man to watch. He seemed destined to surpass his colleagues but tossed it all away by one courageous act of conscience.

Let's set the stage. Conflict was dividing the United States government in the wake of the Civil War. President Andrew Johnson was determined to follow Lincoln's policy of reconciliation toward the defeated South. Congress, however, wanted to rule the downtrodden Confederate states with an iron hand.

Congress decided to strike first. Shortly after Senator Ross was seated, the Senate introduced impeachment proceedings against the hated president. The radicals calculated that they needed 36 votes and smiled as they concluded that the 36th was none other than Ross's.

The new senator listened to the vigilante talk. But to the surprise of many, he declared that the president "deserved as fair a trial as any accused man has ever had on earth." The word immediately went out that his vote was "shaky."

Ross received an avalanche of anti-Johnson telegrams from every section of the country. Radical senators badgered him to "come to his senses."

The fateful day of the vote arrived. The courtroom galleries were packed. Tickets for admission were at an enormous premium. As a death-like stillness fell over the Senate chamber, the vote began. By the time they reached Ross, 24 "guilties" had been announced. Eleven more were certain. Only Ross's vote was needed to oust the president.

The Kansas newspapers and political bosses who had soundly denounced Edmund G. Ross two decades before now praised him for his bold stand against legislative mob rule.

"By the firmness and courage of Senator Ross," it was said, "the country was saved from calamity greater than war, while it consigned him to a political martyrdom, the most cruel in our history. . . . Ross was the victim of a wild flame of intolerance which swept everything before it. He did his duty knowing that it meant his political death.

"It was a brave thing for Ross to do, but Ross did it. He acted for his conscience and with a lofty patriotism, regardless of what he knew must be the ruinous consequences to himself. He acted right."

—John F. Kennedy, *Profiles in Courage* (New York: Harper and Brothers, 1955), 144.

Unable to conceal his emotion, the chief justice asked in a trembling voice, "Mr. Senator Ross, how vote you? Is the respondent Andrew Johnson guilty as charged?"

Ross later explained, at that moment, "I looked into my open grave. Friendships, position, fortune, and everything that makes life desirable to an ambitious man were about to be swept away by the breath of my mouth, perhaps forever."

Then the answer came—unhesitating, unmistakable: "Not guilty!"

With that, the trial was over. And the response was as predicted. A high public official from Kansas wired Ross to say: "Kansas repudiates you as she does all perjurers and skunks."

The "open grave" vision had become a reality. Ross's political career was in ruins. Extreme ostracism and even physical attack awaited his family upon their return home.

One gloomy day Ross turned to his faithful wife and said, "Millions cursing me today will bless me tomorrow . . . though none but God can know the struggle it has cost me." It was a prophetic declaration.

Twenty years later Congress and the Supreme Court verified the wisdom of his position by changing the laws related to impeachment. Ross was appointed territorial governor of New Mexico. Then, just prior to his death, Congress awarded him a special pension. The press and country took this opportunity to honor his courage, which, they finally concluded, had saved the country from crisis and division.

One-Voters, Front and Center

My wife once sent me an interesting greeting card whose front panel read, "We did not make *Who's Who* this year." On the inside were the words "But we're on page 47 of *What Was That?*"

Humbling yet true. Like most people, I consider myself to be a pretty common Joe, a taco-loving, work-resisting, mistake-prone human being. And people like us need to learn lessons from people like us. Does that make sense?

It's easy to think of some of the greatest political leaders of our American past: George Washington, Thomas Jefferson, Abraham Lincoln, Theodore Roosevelt. Their often-repeated acts of courage were impressive.

To be honest, however, I would have to admit that I'm better able to identify with the courage of that lowly senator from Kansas. He had little clout and no pedigree. But he had one vote and used it wisely—and that one vote made a huge difference.

If this is true concerning political courage, it's even more true in relation to Christian courage. On one hand, we rejoice in the courageous lives of biblical celebrities—the well-known, enshrined personalities who were gifted with extraordinary talents or positions. To name a few:

- Esther, the beautiful queen
- David, the musical, handsome leader
- Paul, the captivating speaker
- John, the graphic revelator

On the other hand, many of us learn best from the "nobodies" in God's Word—the ones who cast their "one vote." In each case God used that one vote to make a life-changing difference.[1]

None of these "nobodies" was considered classy, sharp, or of high caliber; they all appeared more seedy than suave. To many of us, they would seem very insignificant—"generic saints."

Yet their stories are a tremendous encouragement to us commoners. Why? Because they have somehow made courage seem attainable in our worlds, in spite of our many limitations and liabilities.

Let us showcase two of these "significant insignificants"—one from the Old Testament and the other from the New. To do so should give us a couple of "courage transfusions."

---

1. See Jon Johnston, *Christian Excellence: Alternative to Success* (Grand Rapids: Baker Book House, 1985), 94-96, for a discussion of little people made big by God. Key point: "God chose (and still chooses) those convinced of their own dependency on Him to confound the proud and powerful; the weak of the world to confound the wise" (see Ezek. 17:24; Zech. 4:6).

A Faith and a Fleece

After 40 hard years of wandering in the desert, it was time to invade the Promised Land. In His final prebattle instructions to Joshua, Israel's commander in chief, God repeated one phrase three times: "Be strong and *courageous*" (Josh. 1:6, 9, see 7, emphasis added).

Perhaps this repetition was necessary. Maybe the leader was hard-of-hearing, senile, or exceedingly nervous. One thing is for sure: Joshua got the message, for he stood strong and courageous during the crucial days that lay ahead.

Joshua sent two spies to Jericho to size up the situation. They ended up at the house of Rahab. Unfortunately, the city's king knew they were there—and was in hot pursuit. What would Rahab do? Turn them over to the authorities and become a local hero? Or protect them and risk her life? It was a big decision for this lowly innkeeper, but one she had to make quickly.

The biblical narrative refers to Rahab as a "prostitute." This reference has caused considerable discussion. Matthew Henry states that she had formerly been of ill repute, had reformed, but could not shed the stigma.

Adam Clarke, on the other hand, contends that harlots and innkeepers were called by the same name: "I am fully satisfied that the term 'zonah' in the text, which has been translated 'harlot,' should be rendered . . . 'inn-keeper' or 'hostess.'"

—*Bethany Parallel Commentary on the Old Testament* (Minneapolis: Bethany House Publishers, 1985), 394.

Rahab dared to listen to her heart. Having heard of the Red Sea miracle and Israel's victory over the Amorites, she realized that Jehovah was the only true God. She recognized that these were His people and that they were *her* people! Rahab courageously abandoned her security and did what was necessary to protect the spies.

Rahab took the men to the rooftop and hid them under a stack of flax. When the authorities came to search, she told them that the men had hit the road. Furthermore, she advised the authorities to chase after the spies. The men liked her idea and were gone in a flash.

That evening Rahab revealed her faith to the spies. With heartfelt sincerity she said, "The LORD your God is God in heaven above and on the earth below" (Josh. 2:11).

Realizing that Israel's forces would be victorious over her city, she then did a very Christian thing: she requested the safety of her family. The spies were aware that Rahab could still turn them in. She had them over a barrel. So they agreed, but with some conditions. At the time of the invasion,

1. A scarlet cord must be tied in the window through which the family would be escaping.
2. Her relatives must be waiting inside her house.
3. The deal was off if she told of their plans.

And with that, the two Israelites were lowered by a rope from the window. After hiding in the hills for three days, they returned to Joshua with their optimistic report and with Rahab's request.

We all know about the famous Battle of Jericho. The walls came down. The city was torched. Every living thing was killed by the sword—*almost* every living thing.

The house bearing the scarlet cord was saved, and Joshua commanded the two spies to usher Rahab and her family to a safe place. Furthermore, they were adopted into the Israelite nation (Josh. 6:20-25).

And that's not all. Rahab actually became an ancestor of our Savior. She married Salmon, father of Boaz, and became a great-great-grandmother of King David. Jesus was born of this same lineage 27 generations later. (See Matt. 1:1-16.)

And to think—all Rahab wanted was to protect her family, to assist those who conquered in the name of the one true God, and to commit her life to Him herself. And God gave her so much more—which is typical of Him.

Rahab's courageous faith earned her very special recognition in God's Word. The writer of Hebrews declares, "By faith the prostitute Rahab, because she welcomed the spies, was not killed with those who were disobedient" (11:31).

Impressive. But let's turn our attention to a New Testament "significant insignificant" whose story has made a deep impact on my life.

Lord, Give Me a Break!

Don't bother looking for any Gothic cathedrals built in his honor. You'll not find him on any list of saints. In fact, his name sounds like some sort of liver disorder.

As for his place in the Bible, he quickly darts in and out—in the space of just nine verses—to perform only one task. But that task was a big assignment from none other than the Lord.

Ananias was very uncertain about the assignment. In fact, he even offered the Lord some background information that just might cause Him to withdraw it. But the Lord knew these details already. He still wanted Ananias to carry through with His request. What was it? Why was it so important? Let's focus on the critical events that led up to this point.

Acts 9 tells us of the most famous conversion story in history. The hot-blooded Pharisee, Saul, had just finished seeing Stephen stoned to death. He had even heard this incredible saint ask the Lord to forgive those who were crushing his bones!

Saul asked himself, "How could a bad man die like that?" In seeking to extinguish this nagging question and his tremendous guilt, he plunged into the most violent action possible. The man from Tarsus bludgeoned believers in Jerusalem. While doing so, he could not help but notice that they remained totally serene. What could possibly give them such inner strength?

In a fanatical frenzy, he stormed to the Sanhedrin to report that he would hunt down Christians who had escaped to Damascus. The Sanhedrin police force accompanied him during the 140-mile, seven-day journey. Because Saul was a Pharisee, however, he would never lower himself to walk with them. Instead, he walked alone.

But that only made matters worse. Alone, he entered into the sanctuary of his deepest thoughts—especially as he trekked through Christ's home turf of Galilee. What sort of magnetism could Jesus possess to attract followers with such unbelievable courage?

Then Paul approached Damascus, described by one as "a handful of pearls in a goblet of emerald." As he descended into the beautiful city, suddenly he was struck blind by a light from heaven. We read about it in Acts 9:

"He fell to the ground and heard a voice say to him, 'Saul, Saul, why do you persecute me?'

"'Who are you, Lord?' Saul asked.

"'I am Jesus, whom you are persecuting,' he replied. 'Now get up and go into the city, and you will be told what you must do'" (vv. 4-6).

The blinded Pharisee rose to his feet and was led by the hand into Damascus. There he neither saw, ate, nor drank for three days. He just poured out his heart to God in continual, repentant prayer.

Now he knew the truth and understood the love of Christians for their Savior. More than anything else, he desired to follow this same Jesus—even if it meant enduring the kind of vicious, unfair persecution he knew of so well.

Still, he asked himself, "Can any Christian forgive me for what I've done? Will any ever accept me as a brother?"

God was already preparing answers to both questions.

In Damascus lived a faithful disciple named Ananias. The Lord said to him, "Go to the house of Judas on Straight Street and ask for a man from Tarsus named Saul, for he is praying. In a vision he has seen a man named Ananias come and place his hands on him to restore his sight" (Acts 9:11-12).

Saul's reputation had preceded him. Ananias had heard of the violence in Jerusalem and knew of Saul's plans to arrest believers in Damascus. He reiterated these facts to the Lord.

But the answer came back, "Go! This man is my chosen instrument to carry my name before the Gentiles and their kings and before the people of Israel" (v. 15).

Case closed. Ananias went, placed his hands on Saul, and said, "*Brother* Saul, the Lord—Jesus, who appeared to you on the road as you were coming here—has sent me so that you may see again and be filled with the Holy Spirit" (v. 17, emphasis added).

"Brother Saul." Notice Ananias's words of warm acceptance and complete forgiveness. No little sermonettes to induce guilt. No demands for an explanation. No judgments of hidden motives. Not even suspicious looks.

God had supplied the instruction to Ananias—so that now all that was left for him to say was "Brother Saul." Those two words said it all.

One commentator calls Ananias "one of the forgotten heroes of the Christian Church."[2] Ananias heard God's instruction and promptly acted at a very critical time—and that took courage.

Surely he wondered if his life would be endangered. And why shouldn't a fellow with Saul's track record be completely ostracized? Was it absolutely necessary to follow through with this mission? If so, why couldn't someone else do it—someone more qualified?

These were questions Ananias never asked. He didn't need to. God's directive to Him superseded all personal misgivings and doubts.

Julius Caesar once boasted, "I came; I saw; I conquered." Ananias went, he saw, and love conquered. Saul was genuinely welcomed as a brother.

How often we hesitate to say "brother" to believers who have a checkered past, don't have the right denominational labels, don't have "enough" years of ecclesiastical seniority, aren't very attractive, say the wrong things, associate with the wrong people, or have no "blue blood genealogy" in the Church.

The warm, forgiving acceptance of Ananias—this courageous "nobody" from Damascus—should put an end to these ways of thinking.

Along with John Wesley, we must declare to every person, "If God is your Father, give me your hand, because you are my brother."

---

2. William Barclay, *Daily Study Bible: The Acts of the Apostles* (Philadelphia: Westminster Press, 1953), 74.

Two insignificants with significant courage: Rahab and Ananias. The first dared to defy her king, risk her life, and accept a new people and their God. The second courageously called a hated persecutor "Brother" and offered him warm acceptance.

Two Tips of a Mammoth Iceberg

The two examples that we chose represent scores who, like them, courageously used their "vote" to make a difference.

In the Old Testament, some favorites come to mind:

False charges against early Christians included the following:
- Bringing calamities (such as earthquakes), because the gods were offended
- Breaking up families—because family deities ceased to be worshiped
- Forsaking old (Jewish) law
- Treating slaves as brothers (such as at the Lord's Supper)
- Being indifferent to property (as in their selling of goods and pooling of resources)
- Resorting to violence (such as in breaking up pagan celebrations)
- Being unpatriotic by not worshiping Caesar
- Becoming atheistic, because they had no material image of their deity

—From class notes of Mendell Taylor at Nazarene Theological Seminary, Kansas City, 1964-67, in a class called "Heritage of the Christian Church."

- *Nathan,* the prophet who rebuked King David for his sin (2 Sam. 12:1-14)
- *Ruth,* who, like Rahab, forsook her homeland and journeyed with her mother-in-law (Naomi) to a strange land (Ruth 1:1-22)
- *Caleb,* 85-year-old conqueror who led Israel's forces into the enemy-infested hill country (Josh. 14:6-14)
- *Mordecai,* Queen Esther's anonymous uncle, who refused to kneel down at the feet of Haman (Esther 3:2)

Likewise, "significant insignificants" surface in the New Testament at critical times to take bold stands. Among them:
- *Joseph,* the simple carpenter who married a young lady pregnant by the Holy Spirit—in spite of public reaction (Matt. 1:18-25)
- *The widow* who courageously put her last coins into the Temple offering (Mark 12:41-44)
- *Lydia,* who offered her home and hospitality to the homeless Paul in Philippi (Acts 16:13-15)
- *Barnabas,* "the encourager" who affirmed Paul at a time when the disciples were hesitant to accept him (Acts 9:26-30)

Throughout the annals of history, common people have taken uncommonly courageous stands—in spite of dungeon, fire, or sword.

One martyr declared, "These are not

chains but ornaments. Though my feet are fettered, my soul is still treading the path to heaven. Earth is shut, but heaven is opening. The world recedes, but paradise receives!"[3]

Millions of courageous Christians today, in countries where Christians are ostracized and physically persecuted, declare the sentiments echoed above. And in other countries many Christians take courageous stands daily. Certainly loss of life is an unlikely threat. But loss of job, marriage, position, wealth, and friendship are ever-present realities.

In fact, hardly a day takes place in any believer's life when courageous stands are not called for. Subtle temptations to compromise are continual and pervasive. Forces within us seem to cause us to grope for moral shortcuts and pathways of least resistance.

We reason that if we were celebrities in the spotlight, we would stand taller. If we were blessed with David's kind of internal strength, we would take on giants. If we lived in a nation of intense persecution for our beliefs, then we would be motivated to boldness. If . . . If . . . If . . .

The message of this chapter is this: We'll never have ideal conditions that will make Christian courage seem attractive, easy, or convenient. There's always a high price to pay—a cross to bear.

But Christ's refreshing presence and His promise of eternal reward make standing tall more than worthwhile—even (especially) if we're common, track-mud-on-the-carpet, onions-with-our-hot-dogs, one-vote people.

And here's something else: We're the very kind of folks—not all that different from Rahab and Ananias—whose courage God uses to make a significant difference. That should give us all a very good feeling and plenty of encouragement.

From People to Principles

It has been jokingly said, "Line up all the philosophers in the world end to end—and you'll never reach a conclusion." By contrast, when we line up all the courageous "significant insignificants" in God's Word, we do reach some conclusions.

From these lives, certain biblical principles emerge that are very relevant to us whoever, wherever, and however we are—right now. For they're timeless and totally reliable.

Let's briefly explore biblical teaching on courage and see how today's Christians measure up.

---

3. From class notes of Mendell Taylor at Nazarene Theological Seminary, Kansas City, 1964-67, in a class called "Heritage of the Christian Church."

6

GOD'S ETERNAL GREEN LIGHT

Even a bad shot is dignified by accepting a duel.

Courage is a diamond with many facets, and it owes much to setting.
—John F. Kennedy

Refuse to . . . drift downstream, gathering debris. . . . Press on.
Without a quest, life is reduced to wimpy black and white,
a diet too bland to get anybody out of bed in the morning.
—Charles Swindoll

I have real problems with two kinds of drivers: "rabbits" and "turtles"—especially at traffic lights.

To have a pedal-to-the-metal speed king run up your back tailpipe is infuriating. You just know that he has a raging case of type-A personality. But to me there's something even worse: being locked in behind distracted or overly cautious "turtles," drivers who seem to take forever to move when the light turns green, the ones who always seem to be there when I'm in a hurry.

The temptation is undeniable. I've wanted to ease up to their bumper and give them a gentle push. Not too hard—just a little encouragement. So far I've managed to resist.

God must have similar frustrations when He sees how hesitantly we move toward taking courageous stands. There we sit in our prolonged stall.

As in most stoplight intersections in America, God provides us with many "green lights" to see. We've looked at two: the chivalrous, holy example of His Son, and the lives of unsung heroes in His Word.

These, and the many saints who have walked (and walk today) in their footsteps, say to all of us, "Go for it—the light's not getting any greener!"

In addition to these living examples, God provides the light of clear, written direction in His Word. This "driver's manual" instructs us in no uncertain terms to be courageous.

No Substitutes, Counterfeits, or Facsimiles

When courage is spoken of in the Old Testament, it usually involves a righteous man admonishing God's people to valiantly and confidently enter battle.

For example, we read in Josh. 10:16-26 that Joshua captured five kings (of Jerusalem, Hebron, Jarmuth, Lachish, and Eglon) in a cave. He summoned all the men of Israel and said to the army commanders, "Come here and put your feet on the necks of these kings" (v. 24). They did.

Then Joshua declared, "Do not be afraid; do not be discouraged. Be strong and courageous. This is what the LORD will do to all the enemies you are going to fight" (v. 25). With that he killed the kings and hanged them on five trees.

By contrast, courage or boldness in the New Testament has many meanings. Let's explore three:

1. *Courage to speak.* The Greek word *parrhēsiazomai* means "to speak boldly or wax bold." Acts 19:8 says, "Paul entered the synagogue and spoke *boldly* there for three months, arguing persuasively about the kingdom of God" (emphasis added). See also Acts 13:46; 18:26; 26:26; 1 Thess. 2:2.

2. *Courage to do.* The Greek word *tolmaō* refers to boldness in undertaking. To the Corinthian church, Paul says: "I beg you that when I come I may not have to be as *bold* as I expect to be toward some people who think that we live by the standards of this world" (2 Cor. 10:2, emphasis added).

3. *Courage to be.* The Greek term *tharreō* implies confidence in one's powers—and it refers to a quality of character. We read in Heb. 13:6, "We say with *confidence*, 'The Lord is my helper; I will not be afraid. What can man do to me?'" (emphasis added).[1]

Though it's very helpful to know how courage is used in the Scriptures, we must press on to grasp the underlying teachings about this necessary Christian virtue.

What are its characteristics? How is it attained? What is its price tag? To these and other important matters we now turn our attention.

Straight Ahead

When we examine the flow of biblical material, several important

---

1. W. E. Vine, "Courage," in *An Expository Dictionary of New Testament Words*, 17th ed. (Old Tappan, N.J.: Fleming H. Revell Co., 1966), 248-49.

principles related to courage seem to emerge. Furthermore, these principles are completely reliable and extremely relevant for us today.

First, our "courage reservoir" builds as we remember how God has brought victory in the past. The war cry "Remember the Alamo" motivated Texas soldiers to recall the Lone Star State's proudest moment and to fight with undaunted courage. It was a shot in the arm to the weary fighters.

Likewise, Israel's deliverance from Egypt echoed in the minds of generations and encouraged them to press forward with boldness. According to the psalmist, when God's people failed, it was because "they forgot the God who saved them, who had done great things in Egypt, miracles in the land of Ham and awesome deeds by the Red Sea" (106:21-22).

All believers can remember times when our Heavenly Father answered in the nick of time. His answer was often not exactly what we expected or requested, but He did answer in the way that was best. Our hindsight assures us of this fact.

We do well to savor such memories and to often recall their glorious details. To do so gives us renewed courage for new battles.

Of course, we must never recall the past to remain there. That would mean a dangerous regression. Rather, our mental return trip must always be for the purpose of gaining courage for the future.

Second, our courage supply increases as we affirm God. The word "affirm" means "to acknowledge worth or to express great confidence in." It's what we do when we cast our ballot on election day or when we exchange wedding rings. For us baseball fans, it's when we yell for the manager to send our favorite player to the plate as a pinch hitter.

We enjoy being encouraged. Pats on the back feel good. But encouragement is even better when someone genuinely affirms us. Why? Because that implies the deepest kind of trust and respect.

God dramatically affirmed Jesus on two important occasions.

1. Just before Jesus began His public ministry, at His baptism God's voice from heaven said, "You are my Son, whom I love; with you I am well pleased" (Mark 1:11).

2. Immediately prior to starting His trip to the Cross, Jesus was affirmed on the Mount of Transfiguration. Again came the voice, this time from a cloud overhead: "This is my Son, whom I love. Listen to him!" (9:7).

Did these affirmations give courage to our Lord? Certainly. After the first, He boldly countered Satan's temptations in the wilderness (Matt. 4:1-11). Following His affirmation on the Mount of Transfiguration, He healed a demon-possessed boy. His disciples wondered why they had been unsuccessful in their attempts.

His reply provided them—and us—with a gold mine of wisdom: "This kind [of demon] can come out only by *prayer*" (Mark 9:29, emphasis added). To understand His response, let's recap a bit.

Our Heavenly Father affirmed Jesus. Those affirmations made Him incredibly courageous. Why? Because He, in turn, constantly affirmed God in prayer. The formula is this:

GA   (*God's Affirmation*)
+ AG   (*Christ's responding Affirmation to God through prayer*)
= C   (*Courage*)

Does this formula work for us? Absolutely. God affirmed us by sending His Son to die for our sins. It was the greatest "I believe in you" message this world has ever known.

Because He lovingly took this initiative, we, like Jesus, have the privilege of affirming Him in prayer. And how, exactly, does our prayer affirm Him? Author and friend Thomas Olbricht explains in his book *The Power to Be*, "Prayer . . . affirm[s] God, because in prayer we confess our dependence on Him and our powerlessness apart from His power."[2]

When we consistently and fervently pray, we acknowledge His value to our lives. The result? Good things happen. We tap into His generous supply of power. Our confidence level rises. Then we become bold. Down deep we know there's nothing God and we can't handle!

Third, the courageous spirit must possess a stalwart faith. Let's do a flashback to Christ's healing of the demon-possessed lad. The father was pleading.

"'If you can do anything, take pity on us and help us.'

"'"If you can"?' said Jesus. '*Everything* is possible for him who believes.'

"Immediately the boy's father exclaimed, 'I do believe; help me overcome my unbelief!'" (Mark 9:22-24, emphasis added).

The son was healed immediately.

Once this burdened father reached out in faith, he no longer complained about the disciples' inefficiency nor looked backward to the details of his child's depressing past. He experienced a genuine attitude adjustment. Words like "expect," "future," "yes," "possible," and "I do" assumed center stage. In short, he assumed a posture of courageous, expectant readiness.

---

2. Thomas H. Olbricht, *The Power to Be: The Lifestyle of Jesus from Mark's Gospel* (Austin, Tex.: Sweet Publishing Co., 1979), 38.

What faith did for this man it has done for many. And it will do the same for us. Let's pause here to refresh ourselves with the words of Heb. 11.

What does it mean to have faith? The Bible declares that "faith is being sure of what we hope for and certain of what we do not see" (v. 1). It's the assurance that comes before the evidence, the smile and the "just you wait and see" look in your eyes.

Faith is the *posture* of courage. Famed philosopher Cicero declared, "A man of courage is also full of faith."

Somebody formed this helpful acrostic with the letters of "faith":

Forsaking
All,
I
Take
Him.

Forsaking all. Abandoning our artificial securities. Breaking loose from past bitterness and doubt. Putting our full weight on His promises. (See Ps. 37:1-8; Prov. 3:5-6.)

One more thing. Prayer and faith work together. Jesus said to His disciples, "Have faith in God" (Mark 11:22). But then He continued, "I tell you, whatever you ask for in prayer, believe that you have received it, and it will be yours" (v. 24).

We must pray in faith—even to the point of thanking God for something that has not yet come to pass. That's not fantasy—it's faith, faith that causes us to arise from our knees with an awesome boldness.

Fourth, courage is often shaped in the fires of trial and persecution. William Barclay translates Rom. 5:3-4 in this way: "We take a pride in our troubles, for we know that trouble produces fortitude, and fortitude produces a character which has stood the test, and character produces hope."

Faith is a word with many meanings. It can mean faithfulness (Matt. 24:45). It can mean absolute trust, as shown by some of the people who came to Jesus for healing (Luke 7:2-10). It can mean confident hope (Heb. 11:1). Or, as James points out, it can even mean a barren belief that does not result in good works (James 2:14-26). What does Paul mean when, in Romans, he speaks of saving faith?

"We must be very careful to understand faith as Paul uses the word, because he ties faith so closely to salvation. It is not something we must do in order to earn salvation. If that were true, then faith would be just one more work, and Paul clearly states that human works can never save us (Gal. 2:16). Instead, faith is a gift God gives us because He is saving us (Eph. 2:8). It is God's grace, not our faith, that saves us. In His mercy, however, when He saves us, He gives us faith—a relationship with His Son that helps us become like Him. Through the faith He gives us, He carries us from death into life (John 5:24).

"Even in Old Testament times grace, not works, was the basis for salvation. As Hebrews points out, 'it is not possible for the blood of bulls and goats really to take away sins' (10:4). God intended for His people to look beyond the animal sacrifices to Him, but all too often they instead put their confidence in fulfilling the requirements of the Law, that is—performing the required sacrifices. When Jesus triumphed over death, He canceled the charges against us and opened the way to the Father (Col. 2:12-15). Because He is merciful, He offers us faith. How tragic if we turn faith into a work and try to develop it on our own! We can never come to God through our own faith, any more than His Old Testament people could come through their own sacrifices. Instead, we must accept His gracious offer with thanksgiving and allow Him to plant the seed of faith in us."

The Greek word for "trouble," *thlipsis*, literally means "pressure." Had a dose of *thlipsis* lately? Some of us seem to have adopted it as our middle name—*Thlipsis* of loneliness, *Thlipsis* of sorrow, *Thlipsis* of unpopularity, *Thlipsis* of persecution.

According to Paul, all of that pressure produces "fortitude," *hupomonē*, which has also been translated "stedfastness" (ASV), "perseverance" (NIV), and "endurance" (SMITH/GOODSPEED).

The picture here is one of gold that has been tried by fire (1 Pet. 1:7). The metal's value is enhanced when the refiner's flames melt away all impurities.

Likewise, the highest form of courage emerges from the fires of adversity. All false and debilitating impurities disappear. Nothing remains but the real thing.

When William Ernest Henley lay in the Edinburgh Infirmary with one leg amputated and the news that the other must follow, he wrote *Invictus*:

> *Out of the night that covers me,*
> *Black as the Pit from pole to pole,*
> *I thank whatever gods may be*
> *For my unconquerable soul.*

Though not recognizing its source as from God, Henley had captured a courage that refused to collapse under the most extreme kind of adversity.

Admittedly, not all persecution produces such a valiant spirit. Just as rainfall makes some ground hard and other soft—depending on the composition of the soil—trial can cause some to become severely embittered, while others are greatly bettered.

If the soil of the heart is right, however, trial can enrich the soul and result in increased courage. In Rom. 5 Paul describes the Christian life that is greatly enhanced by pain. But also one whose "courage quotient" has risen dramatically. This person is not likely to be tripped up by minor, daily frustrations—things that disturb those who have not experienced the fire.

Peter describes what our attitude should be if we're called on to suffer for our Lord. Listen to his gripping words: "Dear friends, do not be surprised at the painful trial you are suffering, as though something strange were happening to you. But rejoice that you participate in the sufferings of Christ, so that you may be overjoyed when his glory is revealed. . . . If you suffer as a Christian, do not be ashamed, but praise God that you bear that name" (1 Pet. 4:12-13, 16).

Fifth, as we act courageously, we must become averse to the spotlight. Piety parades are detestable to the Lord. In no uncertain words He declares, "Be careful not to do your 'acts of righteousness' before men, to be seen by them. If you do, you will have no reward from your Father in heaven" (Matt. 6:1).

Courage can easily become an exhibition virtue. Because it's so universally admired, we're tempted to show it off to others—so that others will eat their hearts out with envy or treat us with inordinate amounts of respect.

But courage must never become a display, in spite of how much we've had to pray and suffer to attain it and what God has helped us to accomplish because of it. Our courage must be a secret between us and God. To parade it would be to

- take credit for something He gave us
- place ourselves in the precarious domain of pride
- receive our reward on earth rather than in heaven (Matt. 6:1)

Even His enemies realized that Jesus was extremely courageous. One day they admitted to Him, "Teacher, we know you are a man of integrity. You aren't swayed by men, because you pay no attention to who they are; but you teach the way of God in accordance with the truth" (Mark 12:14).

Jesus did not even thank them for the compliment. He was not about to take a bow and tell them that they were good judges of character. Why? Because He knew they were not sincere. And even if they had been, His interest was not in fame, publicity, or starting a hero cult. Rather, it was exemplifying servanthood to the poor in spirit—those who were guaranteed to do zilch for His career!

When Beethoven heard about his encroaching deafness, particularly traumatic for a musician, he said, "I will take life by the throat." When Sir Walter Scott became bankrupt because his publishers went broke, he declared, "No man will say 'Poor fellow!' to me; my own right hand will pay the debt!" Another gallant person, undergoing great sorrow, was told, "Sorrow colors your life, doesn't it?" His reply was, "Yes. That it does. But I intend on choosing the colors!" All of these are illustrations of *hupomonē.*

—William Barclay, *The Daily Study Bible: The Letter to the Romans* (Philadelphia: Westminster Press, 1957), 70.

〜✺〜

Another good reason for not boasting about our courage: Our audience may contain people who have been far more courageous than we have. I heard the story about a man who came through the famous Johnstown (Pennsylvania) flood and enjoyed telling about every one of his heroics. The fellow finally died, met Peter, and immediately requested an audience to relate his well-rehearsed story. Peter declared, "Of course. It will be arranged at once. But there's just one thing you may wish to know—Noah will be in your audience."

For many of us, this biblical advice is a pretty big pill to swallow. We compete to attain power, privileges, prestige, and possessions. If we win and gain advantages over others, we're quick to make our victories visible: a "better" selection of friends, designer products, more expensive vacations.

Courage is a virtue that's not attained easily. It's a rare trophy, a merit of honor, something that singles us out, making us seem very distinctive. But the Bible tells us to keep our "courage medal" in the dresser drawer, to destroy our "courage scrapbook," to relinquish all "bragger's rights" to courageous feats we've performed.

Our courage is from Christ, and to Him the credit must return—that is, for now. Someday, if we've been content with incognito courage in this world, we'll receive a reward that's unimaginably glorious. Paul says so. Recalling Isa. 64:4, he writes, "No eye has seen, no ear has heard, no mind has conceived what God has prepared for those who love him" (1 Cor. 2:9).

This is one prize worth waiting for—and worth keeping a secret for!

So Why the Hesitation?

The Bible speaks of courage in an up-front, clear manner. The principles stated above are repeatedly revealed in stories and doctrinal teachings. To miss them is to ignore them on purpose.

We're all at an intersection with hundreds of green lights and a sea of beckoning fingers encouraging us to proceed toward the attainment of godly courage. Some of us won't budge. We remain immobilized in a dead stall. Others of us resemble Sunday drivers. We move out very slowly and poke along—becoming hazardous to ourselves and everyone else.

Both of these miss the meaning of the green light. God has sent a definite message. He expects us to "step on it," to move along deliberately, purposely, and with expectation. Courage will not simply come to us as we sit and wait. We must, prayerfully and with faith, move toward it in spite of the risks. Why? Because there's really no other way to be obedient to Him.

So why do we linger? There are many possible answers:

1. We're overcome by a paralyzing *fear*. John Wesley said, "Fear

freezes and benumbs the soul." But Paul said, "God hath not given us the spirit of fear; but of power, and of love, and of a sound mind" (2 Tim. 1:7, KJV).

2. Our attachment to, or dependence on, some *authority figure* keeps us from venturing forth. An anonymous person spoke the truth when he or she said, "In the final essence, Jesus is the only One who can control your life without destroying it."

3. Many of us are crippled by a *sheep complex*. With invisible antennae, we continuously scan to determine what the crowd is thinking. Then we follow along to avoid rejection. Romans admonishes, "Be not conformed to this world" (12:2, KJV).

4. Others of us have an acute case of *psychic overload*. Like overtaxed computers, we have too many demands on our system. We feel as if we're flooded, pulled in all directions, unable or unwilling to clearly focus on doing what we need to do.

5. More than a few of us depend on *crisis motivation*. We have an inoperable self-starter. We must be forced by an emergency to be courageous. Otherwise, we slump back into lethargy or fantasy.

6. A good number of us are *shovelers*. Rather than responding with gallant boldness, we say to ourselves, "Let someone else do it. Why should I get involved?" We shovel our responsibilities onto others.

7. Many of us have *"spectator-itis."* We're so involved in admiring other courageous persons that we neglect our own responsibilities. Biblical courage is not meant to be a spectator sport!

8. Finally, great numbers of us have an acute case of *"heart void."* Because we've never experienced God's Spirit in our beings, we lack the necessary inner strength to be courageous.

Society overloads us with an excessive number of responsibilities. As a result, our concern turns to stress. Why? Because our minds are unable to process the number of demands. T. H. Holmes and R. H. Rahe tell us that our constitution can take only so much overload. Beyond that point, a deterioration of emotional or physical health is likely. Furthermore, our relationships are apt to suffer. This is why persons contracting debilitating illnesses often get divorced, or why parents who lose a child frequently turn on each other. Inordinate quantities of unprocessed overload cause many to search for scapegoats.

See the Holmes-Rahe chart of "life events" and the corresponding amounts of stress that each is likely to cause in Jon Johnston's *Walls or Bridges: How to Build Relationships That Glorify God* (Grand Rapids: Baker Book House, 1988), 237-39.

According to a biochemist colleague, scientific studies indicate that some people are addicted to their own adrenaline. These individuals have a track record of being motivated only by crisis.

The crisis scares them, which causes their body's defense system to manufacture adrenaline. This in turn is their "fuel for motivation." But without the presence of that fuel, they're listless and immobile.

Wesleyan Arminians refer to a "second work of grace," or "entire sanctification." During the initial, born-again experience, God forgives the sins of the past. He pardons the sinner. But then God's Word and the Holy Spirit beckon the believer to a second experience—a time when the Holy Spirit instantaneously cleanses original sin from the heart, when the pardoned rebel consecrates his or her life and receives purity and the power to witness boldly.

It's highly unlikely that Jesus' disciples would remain as unpardoned sinners. Their encounters with Him were too intense for that possibility. Though immature, they were not rebels. They loved their

These appear to be some of the primary reasons why we don't mobilize ourselves in response to God's green lights, why we refuse to experience joys of courage.

But there is another group that's perhaps much larger. And it's to this multitude that the remainder of this book is directed.

Busy Firemen?

My friend is a firefighter in Kansas City. The vast majority of firefighters are, no doubt, very courageous like my friend. When flames are leaping out of a 12-floor apartment house, and trapped people are screaming deliriously, most firemen hurriedly rush inside for the rescue.

According to my friend, though, there are a few who fail to respond in this manner. When lives are at stake, and seconds are of critical importance, they busy themselves with trivial tasks like straightening hoses, checking out ladder joints, engaging in conversation—anything and everything except courageously rushing up the ladder to save lives.

No doubt, like most of us, these persons are courageous in some areas of their lives: arguing with their spouses, haggling with their bosses for a raise, bullying someone while driving on the freeway, taking a defective product back to the store.

Sure, they're courageous, all right—but in areas of small and or negative consequence —compared to charging into burning buildings to rescue victims. One might figuratively put it this way: many are "busy playing marbles rather than firing cannons." They're immersed in trifles, bogged down in making courageous stands on "Who cares?" issues.

As Christians, we're strongly admonished to be courageous on issues that are near and dear to the heart of God, issues that are very likely to be ignored by most people —even those who are considered "courageous."

We'll explore these issues in Part 3.

Master and sought to learn His ways. They were definitely born again.

But after Jesus' death came the Pentecostal experience, when "all of them were filled with the Holy Spirit" (Acts 2:4). Result: They were purified, and their newfound courage was amazing. (Compare Peter's boldness in Acts 3 with his denials of Christ prior to the Crucifixion.)

Part 3

COURAGE—
HOW CAN WE BEST EXPRESS IT?

7

CROSS MY HEART AND HOPE TO DIE

COURAGE IS INTEGRITY

*Heroes are made every little while, but only one in a million
conduct themselves afterwards so that it makes us proud that
we honored them at the time.*
—Will Rogers

*I believe that every right implies a responsibility,
every opportunity an obligation, every possession a duty.*
—John D. Rockefeller Jr.

*No wrong choice . . . can persuade God to love you less.
Believe this, and you will have new courage to make choices,
even when you are not sure they [are] the right ones.*
—Lewis B. Smedes

A lady once declared, "I don't know what this world is coming to. Someone stole my good Holiday Inn towels right off my clothesline!" We smile only because we're reminded of our own ethical inconsistencies, the times when our integrity seems to vanish—such as when we

- indulge in some dubious "pencil magic" on our income taxes
- underestimate our vehicular velocity to a traffic judge
- view X-rated movies while alone in a hotel in a distant city
- give our "afflicted" car a verbal clean bill of health to a prospective buyer
- become a flirtatious playmate with someone other than our spouse
- "forget" to turn in a valuable object that we found

Most of us talk a good game. Lying, cheating, stealing—we say they're repulsive to us. We say we want to be isolated from those who indulge in such moral calamities. Most of us mean what we hear ourselves saying. Our intentions seem pure enough.

73

Then with about as much warning as an electrical blackout, tempta-tion rears its ugly head. We're faced with making decisions. We must choose between right and wrong or, more difficult yet, between *shades* of right.

All too often our emotions end up winning the tug-of-war with our willpower. We take the way of least resistance—the shortcut, the way that promises to yield the most personal benefit—in spite of who gets hurt or cheated.

A Trio of Conscience Tests

Bags of cash once tumbled from an armored truck in Columbus, Ohio. A month or two later, the same thing occurred in San Francisco and Toronto. In all cases, most of the money was grabbed by passersby.

The Ohio episode in particular was a unique test of reaction to unex-pected riches. A massive traffic jam was created by motorists who stopped to scoop up $2 million worth of bills scattered by the wind.

Only $100,000 was returned. And many of those who brought the money back received no praise. Mel Kiser, an Ohio Bell repairman who re-turned $57,000, said, "My mother said she was proud of me—that that's the way she trained me. But my dad said, 'I thought I raised you better than that!'"

This strange event is a mirror reflecting our nation's commitment to integrity. Study the scenario. Only one-twentieth of the money was re-turned. Those who stepped forward to relinquish their findings were con-sidered by many to be fools.

You may say, "But it's always been that way. Since year one, human be-ings have been pretty shady characters who do what it takes to gain personal advantage." In a real sense, that's right. Abraham Lincoln, who walked miles to return six cents to a customer who overpaid, was an exception, for his era as well as our own.

So why speak of a depletion of integrity in the present? As author James Dobson writes, "Sin is nothing new. Telling lies, welshing on prom-ises, being unfaithful, cheating on taxes, are not unique to our day. And they surely cannot be laid at the clay feet of an overgeneralized 'social de-cay.' However . . . through my travels, I do get the overpowering sense that the expression of these evils appears to be increasing. Increasing numbers of well-meaning but naive citizens are placing themselves and their fami-lies in moral jeopardy."[1]

---

1. James Dobson's foreword in Ted W. Engstrom, *Integrity* (Waco, Tex.: Word Books, 1987), ix-x.

Take this nation's schools, for instance. In previous times mischief was tolerated—but not malfeasance; high spirits were accepted—but not low deeds. Today in urban schools it's the very brave (and endangered) teacher who reprimands malicious abuse, theft, or lying.[2]

Consider the professional world. We hear sordid accounts of sports stars involved in sexual affairs, financiers attempting cloak-and-dagger deals, social scientists reporting spurious findings, politicians receiving slush funds from corporations, and televangelists enmeshed in all of the above—and more. Today almost every job seems to have an undertow of powerful temptations that pulls us away from integrity.

And along with these, we have plenty of tailor-made rationalizations to whitewash our questionable deeds. We've all heard (or used) them:

"I'm only doing what's necessary to survive."

"In this day it's expected."

"It won't really hurt anybody."

"I'm doing it for my wife and children."

"It's my own way of getting back at the system."

Because our societal fabric is not woven with strong, ethical fibers, those of us with integrity must have a lion's share of moral courage.

To be such a person is commendable indeed. Alexander Pope put it well: "An honest man is the noblest work of God."

But to understand what's involved in becoming such a stalwart, let's explore some dimensions contained in the appealing quality that we call "integrity." There's more here than meets the

---

Author Dale Evans Rogers presents the following results of a survey of 2,000 high school seniors in California:

- **75 percent admitted to copying from another's exam (most did it repeatedly).**
- **73 percent owned up to using cribnotes to cheat on exams.**
- **51 percent confessed to copying, word for word, from books—and presenting it as their own ideas.**
- **97 percent said they have witnessed others cheating on exams.**
- **42 percent claimed there are some "very good reasons for cheating," like making high grades for college entrance and an eventual high-paying career.**
- **Only 1 percent declare they would report a friend they saw cheating.**

—David O. Savage, "High School Test Cheating: 75 Percent Admitted Cite Pressure," *Los Angeles Times*, April 7, 1986, Part 1, page 3; summarized in Dale Evans Rogers' *Only One Star: A Cure for the Celebrity Syndrome* (Dallas: Word Publishing, 1988), 128.

---

2. Marya Mannes, "Dad, What's a Conscience?" *Newsweek*, April 15, 1974, 11.

eye. And it's of great relevance in the family room as well as the classroom, the boardroom as well as the bedroom.

Comprehending the "I" Word

Put very simply, *integrity* comes from the word *integer*. It implies being whole, indivisible, and singular. In short, it's a single-hearted mind-set.[3]

Integrity is being true-blue, rock-ribbed, straight shooting, credible, on the level, non-fictitious. When we have integrity, there's an internal-external consistency. What we say, we mean. What we seem to be, we are. What we talk, we walk.

But that's the ideal. Most of us appear to be somewhat downrange on the integrity continuum. Lawrence Kohlberg, a Harvard psychologist, has pinpointed six plateaus of moral development. Let's venture a guess as to where we're located.

Like Swiss child psychologist Jean Piaget, Kohlberg believes that the ability to reason about moral problems develops by stages. Morally, a child must "crawl" before he or she can "walk." Kohlberg's basic premise is that moral development, like intellectual development, is a natural process that teachers can nurture in children.

Furthermore, these stages are based on the maturation of the mind. State one is typical of children up to age seven. Stage two is found in preadolescents. Stage three is characteristic of adolescents. Stage four is the one in which most people remain.

He asserts that each stage in moral reasoning is psychologically and philosophically more mature than the previous stage. Thus, he terms the first two stages "preconventional morality," because they are dominated by the child's egocentric needs and desires. The second two are labeled "conventional morality," because

---

Stage one: obedience and punishment. Right is what authorities command. The underlying motive is fear of punishment, not respect for authority or values.

Stage two: back-scratching. People begin to seek a return for their favors. It's the "I'll do for you but only if you reciprocate" mentality. Kohlberg terms it "the morality of the marketplace."

Stage three: conformity. Good behavior is what pleases or helps others and is what they approve. The evaluations and expectations of peers are particularly strong.

Stage four: law and order. What's right is doing one's duty, showing respect for authority, and maintaining the given social or-

---

3. Engstrom, *Integrity,* book jacket copy.

der. What the law commands transcends all other considerations.

Stage five: social contract. Right is defined in terms of the general rights of individuals, as agreed upon by the whole society (for example, the United States Constitution).

Stage six: universal principles. Morality is based on decisions of conscience made in accordance with self-chosen principles of right—principles that are universal and consistent.

they are based on a recognition of the rules laid down by society. Finally, the last two stages are termed "postconventional morality," because they are rooted in principles of justice by which the individual judges himself or herself, other people, and society.

—Kenneth L. Woodward, "Moral Education," *Newsweek*, March 1, 1976, 74.

According to the psychologist, most of us never rise above stage four. We're obsessed with our own rights under the law. We're not really concerned about how our actions impact the rights of others (stage five). Nor can we even relate with those—like Gandhi, Socrates, Mother Teresa— who followed their consciences regardless of the cost (stage six).

To the Victor Goes the Reward!

Though rare to find in its purest form, and though it demands great courage, integrity is worthy of our pursuit.

For one thing, it does wonders for us. Realizing this fact, Edgar Guest offers this thought-provoking poem:

Myself

I have to live with myself, and so
I want to be fit for myself to know,
I want to be able, as days go by,
Always to look myself straight in the eye;
I don't want to stand, with the setting sun,
And hate myself for the things I've done.

I don't want to keep on a closet shelf
A lot of secrets about myself,
And fool myself, as I come and go,
Into thinking that nobody else will know
The kind of a man I really am;
I don't want to dress up myself in sham.

I want to go out with my head erect,
I want to deserve all men's respect;

But here in the struggle for fame and pelf
I want to be able to like myself.
I don't want to look at myself and know
That I'm bluster and bluff and empty show.

I can never hide myself from me;
I see what others may never see;
I know what others may never know;
I never can fool myself, and so,
Whatever happens, I want to be
Self-respecting and conscience free.[4]

Again, a primary benefactor of our integrity is ourselves. This is true not only of life but also of memories that linger beyond our mortal existence.

Respected minister Charles H. Spurgeon wrote, "A good character is the best tombstone. Those who loved you, and were helped by you, will remember you when forget-me-nots are withered. Carve your name on hearts, and not on marble."[5]

That's integrity, a better long-term investment than the best certificate of deposit available!

In addition to ourselves, our integrity has a wholesome ripple effect on those around us. With every act of honesty and every expression of authentic credibility, people feel affirmed and encouraged about humanity. Furthermore, the level of trust begins to rise—replacing the rampant looking-out-for-number-one mentality of our day. Muscles relax. Smiles appear. Anxiety lessens.

In his book *Integrity*, Ted Engstrom writes, "When we can no longer depend on one another or do what we said we would do, the future becomes an undefined nightmare."[6]

In our day of specialization and automation, it's imperative that we have mutual trust. Our doctors must be trusted when they operate on our bodies. Our pilots must be trusted when they're landing the airplanes we're traveling on. Our bankers must be trusted with our life savings. Our ministers must be trusted when they "rightly divid[e] the word of truth" (2 Tim. 2:15, KJV).

Once again, with every deed of integrity comes an elevation in the lev-

---

4. From "The Collected Verse of Edgar A. Guest," by Edgar A. Guest. © 1984. Used by permission of NTC/Contemporary Publishing Group, Inc.
5. Engstrom, *Integrity*, 67.
6. Ibid., 2

el of trust. Result: our world is made a better place, one in which people can be reconciled to one another in peace and love.

Third, in addition to ourselves and others, the Lord considers our integrity as an important form of worship. We honor Him and reflect His very nature when we're morally upright. That's why His Word has so much to say about integrity.

It Jumps Out at Us

The Bible is replete with appeals for integrity. Even the slowest of learners is able to grasp the importance our Heavenly Father attributes to this virtue. After Solomon completed the Temple and royal palace, God said to him, "As for you, if you walk before me in *integrity* of heart and uprightness . . . I will establish your royal throne over Israel forever" (1 Kings 9:4-5, emphasis added).

The psalmist declares, "Judge me, O LORD, according to my righteousness, according to my *integrity*, O Most High" (7:8, emphasis added). Again he writes, "May *integrity* and uprightness protect me, because my hope is in you" (25:21, emphasis added). Then he testifies, "In my *integrity* you uphold me and set me in your presence forever" (41:12, emphasis added).

In Proverbs we're told that God "holds victory in store for the *upright*, he is a shield to those whose walk is blameless" (2:7, emphasis added). How about this one? "The *integrity* of the upright guides them, but the unfaithful are destroyed by their duplicity" (11:3, emphasis added). Sooner or later comes a day of reckoning.

Perhaps few people ever lived with more integrity than Job. The Bible describes him as "blameless and upright" (1:1). Does that mean he was patient in the sense of being uncomplaining? Not exactly. It seems as though only David out-complained Job.

Then how was his integrity manifested?

1. *He had a right relationship with God.* We're told that he "feared God and shunned evil" (1:1).
2. *He lived a righteous life in his community.* People who knew him thought of him as "blameless and upright."
3. *He was characterized by faithfulness and steadfastness.* In the midst of incomprehensible physical and mental torture, he declared, "Though he slay me, yet will I hope in him" (13:15). "I know that my Redeemer lives" (19:25).[7]

---

7. This outline was taken from an October 1988 chapel address at Trevecca Nazarene University, Nashville, given by former president Homer J. Adams.

Jesus describes Nathanael as a person "in whom there is nothing false" (John 1:47). Are there any of us who would not give everything we own to hear our Lord say that about us?

And how about Christ's integrity? He always spoke the unvarnished truth, and in direct, simple words. That's why He forbade oath taking and said, "Simply let your 'Yes' be 'Yes,' and your 'No,' 'No'" (Matt. 5:37). For us as believers, our word must *be* our oath.

We live in a world in which style seems more important than substance, in which oaths are required in courts so people will feel obligated to tell the truth, in which speakers operate under the motto "If you can't dazzle 'em with brilliance, baffle 'em with confusion."

Jesus manifested integrity in so many other ways. He called the leaders in Jerusalem liars, blind men, fools, serpents, vipers. He refused to display a fake humility by concealing His extraordinary knowledge. He warned people that they were moving toward perdition and painted their ruin in words that cause the human heart to shudder.

Since Jesus' earthly existence, many uncomplimentary things have been said about our Lord. But even His harshest critics have hesitated to call Him an intentional deceiver. They have said He was mistaken, called Him a visionary, fanatic, and dreamer—but not a person capable of telling a lie. As Charles Edward Jefferson so aptly put it, "There is something so pure and frank and noble about Him that to doubt His sincerity would be like doubting the brightness of the sun."[8]

So the evidence is overwhelming. A thread of integrity connects the earliest biblical patriarchs with the life of our sinless Savior, with Christians who have lived since then until our present day. The words and tempo of this great "biblical hymn" may vary throughout time, but the song is essentially the same.

Unfortunately, not all who claim to live by biblical principles are singing this "song"—or, if they are, they're singing off-key. And that should concern all of us, just as it concerns our Lord.

You Call It!

Question: Do you have Christian friends who seem a little flaky when it comes to being up-front and honest, persons who do or say things you really wonder about?

Something really bothers me, and I might as well confess it. I frequently observe those who claim no allegiance to biblical teaching—but who

---

8. Jefferson, *Character of Jesus*, 63-64.

manifest impeccable integrity. On the other hand, I'm perplexed by ethical practices of some who profess to be ardent followers of Jesus.

I know what you're thinking: "Yes, but sinners are ethically upright for the wrong reasons. Morality is their religion or crutch." No doubt there's truth to that. But does that let the suspect Christians off the hook?

Allow me to share three brief illustrations, which will give a better idea of what I'm getting at.

Illustration number one. A couple I know are both leaders in their church. They're faithful in attendance, tithe their income, know hymns by heart, close their eyes while praying. In general, they're thought to be A-OK laypersons.

In all ways they're pretty typical. Sure—like all of us, they have their idiosyncrasies. The lady is known to be fairly close with money. She spends plenty of time at flea markets and garage sales. And—can you believe this? —she requires that her children use no more than two squares of toilet tissue at a time! Oh, well—I guess we all have our quirks.

But this couple frequently takes their family on weekend jaunts in their camper. And when they do, they think nothing of pulling up to a Holiday Inn, sneaking past the swimming pool gate, and taking a dip that lasts for several hours.

Notice that I said they "sneak," which implies knowledge of wrongdoing. And when inside, they're confronted with signs declaring, THIS POOL IS RESTRICTED TO PATRONS STAYING IN OUR MOTEL.

Now, in describing these experiences to us, this couple seems to pass off their actions as clever, innocent fun. I just wonder if their children sneak into the hotel bathrooms to experience the pleasure of using sufficient quantities of toilet paper!

Illustration number two. Like most of you, I hold ministers in the highest regard. There's something very special about those who have dedicated their lives to professional ministry. But once a minister approached my wife and me as we were having a cup of tea at an evangelism conference. This very prominent clergyman brought up the issue of hotel rates. Knowing that we travel a great deal, he proceeded to brag about his gimmick.

In order to stay at the best places, at a fraction of the regular cost, this guy had cards printed that gave the impression that he was a bona fide travel agent. And the front desk personnel never questioned his claim. As a result, his church was saved a nice chunk of money.

His second ingenious idea was requested of my wife, who is a travel consultant. The minister asked her to secure two airline tickets. But his request included something that didn't seem quite ethical. He realized that staying over Saturday night cuts most fares significantly, but he knew that neither of his trips included a layover.

A clever thought occurred to him: Why not simply put the two halves together? Then it would appear as though the Saturday night requirement had been satisfied on both trips.

Well, he spelled out his scheme to my wife, who suffers from an overactive conscience. She was uncomfortable about the idea and checked it out with her boss. Sure enough, she was told that if the airlines caught wind of the minister's plan, he could be in serious difficulty.

It was embarrassing, but she had to do it—she phoned the minister and kindly told him that his request could not be granted. His comment: "But I hear of other ministers doing it all the time!"

Illustration number three. Those of us who have spent time on a college campus realize how important it is for faculty members to earn their doctoral degrees. Without one, they're made to feel about as welcome as a cat at a mouse convention.

At one Christian college I know of, a certain doctorateless professor decided that he could take no more psychological abuse. He had endured insults and lower salary for 15 years, and that was long enough. It was high time for him to receive acceptance!

He traveled to a distant city and enrolled in a diploma mill program. After paying a handsome amount, filling out a few papers, and taking a few superficial courses, he was granted his Mickey Mouse diploma.

The next week he slapped the impressive certificate on the desk of his dean and proudly declared himself an authentic doctor. It was promptly announced, and congratulations poured in. Not incidentally, he received the long-awaited substantial increase in salary.

Then it happened. It was either a one-in-a-million happenstance or, more likely, the providence of God. The chairman of his discipline somehow ran into an official from the counterfeit school. As they conversed, he was aghast as the latter described the school's laughable requirements. Finally, the beans were spilled, as the make-believe administrator revealed the identity of the mutually recognized professor.

The chairman was stunned. How could his trusted faculty member attempt such a ridiculous stunt? He must be out of his mind!

You can anticipate the remainder of the story. The professor was confronted, then promptly and unceremoniously fired. Furthermore, his college reviewed the painful lesson they had learned.

I've always wondered if the guy sent back his diploma and requested a refund. Here's a better idea: Maybe he should have been made to return tuition money to his students!

Let us pause long enough to recap the reasons given for the improprieties described in the preceding illustrations:

Illustration number one—*having innocent fun.*

Illustration number two—*saving the church money; and "other ministers are doing it."*

Illustration number three—*achieving acceptance and respectability.*

Well, what's your verdict? Are these legitimate and acceptable? Perhaps we're in danger of taking this integrity business too far? Maybe we should not insist on high ethical standards that seem to so many to be unreasonable and even unattainable?

My Ongoing Battle

I must confess my own difficulty in meeting the rigorous standard of integrity. Convenience deceptions are a continual temptation—especially

- when the unvarnished, bold truth appears to be too much for some to handle (such as persons who are emotionally explosive, terminally ill, or new to the faith)
- when it's a matter of giving someone credit for a thought he or she originated but which I expounded on in my writing (sure, I end up doing it, but sometimes quite begrudgingly)
- when my loophole-conscious tax man encourages me to be excessively generous in estimating certain expenses
- when a student with a mediocre academic record but a winsome personality requests me to write a positive letter of recommendation
- when the Concord grapes look so delicious and tasty in our local supermarket, and I'm tempted to sample a few

Then there's money. My problem seems to arise when I feel that I'm being unfairly assessed—as in the time we bought our first house. Getting enough for a down payment required a complete exhaustion of our meager monetary supply. To put it bluntly, we were broke. Busted.

In determining the amount of loan we needed, all escrow fees were figured in. It appeared to be a neat package.

Well, a year later the telephone rang. It was the escrow company. They had discovered a miscalculation on their part. I owed them $1,000.

Have you ever had a rush of 12 different emotions at once? Then you know how I felt. But the predominant feeling corresponded to my basic thought, namely, that I did not owe them a dime!

It was their mistake. They admitted it. No court could possibly stick me with some dated fee that an escrow company retrieved from left field. I would ignore the call and the whole matter. Period.

Unfortunately, it was not really a period. It was more like a comma. My conscience tape began to roll on its own. And its "off" button wouldn't work—no matter how hard I pushed it.

I said to myself, "I'll put this whole thing to rest by getting confirmation from my friends." They heard my explanation and, predictably, sided with my decision. That was it—time to close the file drawer.

But the file drawer wouldn't stay closed. And I was driven to ask myself the only question that really matters: "Do I owe the money?"

I felt certain that a quick review of the figures would demonstrate their error. So I retrieved the sheets and used my calculator. Then came the bottom line reality: I did, in fact, owe the money. They had made an honest mistake.

With that, I telephoned the company and asked to speak to the president. He listened intently as I explained my situation. I hoped that my sincerity would cause him to excuse the whole matter.

His response: "Sorry about our mistake, but you really do owe the money."

Now why did he have to use *that* choice of words? It only added to my discomfort.

Then I realized that God had me cornered. I simply had to pay the money—money we really didn't have.

As my conversation with the president continued, I detected a note of compassion in his voice. After telling him that I was a Christian who wanted to do the right thing, his position softened. Result: He agreed that a $500 payment would be sufficient.

I sent the money. The tape recorder of my conscience stopped playing. The file drawer closed. And down deep I felt good.

Should I have returned the money? Was I obeying a biblical principle, or simply being driven by an overly sensitive, misdirected conscience? You be the judge.

But regardless of your verdict, we can agree on one thing: biblical integrity *is* essential plainly and simply—for our inner peace and for our Christian witness.

And because our world manifests such an extreme shortage of this crucial spiritual quality, perhaps it's quite permissible for us to go a little overboard in demonstrating it.

8

Your Heartbreak in Me

COURAGE IS COMPASSION

---

*Conservative: someone who throws a 25-foot rope to a drowning man
50 feet away and says, "Swim for it; it'll build character."
Liberal: a person who throws a 50-foot rope to a drowning man
25 feet away, then walks away to do another "good deed."*

*Must one point out that from ancient times a decline in courage
has been considered the beginning of the end?*
—Aleksandr Solzhenitsyn

*Granted, if we go His way, we will be broken;
but if we don't, we will be crushed.*
—Mel Rich

To understand compassion, it's helpful to examine its opposite—cruelty. Many songs tell about cruel people. Certain occupations are reputed to attract persons with ice water in their veins.

I heard about a lawyer whose yacht sank in a pool of sharks. As he swam for safety, the man-eaters immediately parted to let him through—they considered it a professional courtesy.

And then there's a man who prepared to have a heart transplant. His doctors asked him to choose between two available hearts: one from a young athlete, the other from a middle-aged college dean. To their surprise, he promptly chose the dean's, saying, "It'll last me much longer, because it probably hasn't ever been used."

Speaking of the heartless, perhaps there are few who are considered more callous than win-driven high school football coaches. One afternoon, during a brutal scrimmage in 90-degree heat, my quarterback friend was flattened by a red-dogging linebacker who nailed him from his blind side. There he lay on the turf, racked with intense pain. His "compassionate"

m

As leaders, Herod and Jesus have been contrasted in these ways:

Herod	Jesus
selfish	compassionate
murderer	Healer
immoral	just and good
political opportunist	Servant
king over small territory	King over all creation

—*Life Application Study Bible*, s.v. "Herod." Copyright © 1988, by Tyndale House Publishers, Inc., Wheaton, Illinois 60189. All rights reserved. Used by permission.

coach walked over to where he was lying, looked down at him, and snarled, "Don't mash my grass!"

Even a cursory look at history reveals a plethora of monstrous rulers who concurred with a principle put down by 16th-century philosopher Niccolò Machiavelli, namely, "It is better for leaders to be feared than to be loved."

One such person was King Herod (47-4 B.C.), who constructed Jerusalem's Temple. He was a generous man, having melted down his own gold dinner plate to buy corn for starving countrymen. But he was insane with suspicion. Anyone suspected as a rival was permanently eliminated.

We all know that Herod attempted to kill the Baby Jesus—by annihilating all of Bethlehem's male infants (Matt. 2:7-18). He murdered his wife, Mariamne, and dipped her in honey. He also assassinated his mother-in-law, Alexandra, and his older son, Antipater. Not wanting to show favoritism, he wiped out his other two sons, Alexander and Aristobulus.

Herod's savage, warped nature is vividly seen in his arrangements for his own death. Told that his 70-year-old body was being eaten by worms, he went to his spacious Jericho palace to die. Immediately he gave orders to arrest Jerusalem's most distinguished citizens on trumped-up charges.

Then he instructed that these people must be slaughtered the moment he died. Why? His sick mind reasoned that nobody would ever mourn for him—but if these people were butchered on the day of his death, that would guarantee sympathy throughout the land.[1]

Herod was cruel, as were scores of other leaders throughout the history of humanity. But what does this barbarism have to do with us?

Offensive Unit on the Field!

Today we hear about a continuous flow of crime in our cities and of people's tempers getting out of hand at places like sporting events, expressways, and airline reservation desks.

---

1. William Barclay, *Daily Study Bible Series: The Gospel of Matthew* (Philadelphia: Westminster Press, 1956), 19-20.

But most of us don't react so harshly and irresponsibly. We're basically decent persons who find it difficult to kill a June bug or to turn down a Girl Scout selling cookies.

Commendable? Perhaps. But Jesus demands more, much more. His Word calls on us to take the initiative for right—not only to refrain from being cruel, but also to lovingly reach out to those who have been victimized.

We're to act this way even when it seems foolish. And we must reach out in love even when it's inconvenient—which is most of the time. These actions require a kind of courage that many of us naturally shy away from.

But sometimes we see glimpses of such chivalry, and when we do, it refreshes and inspires us. There's the New York family who combined their efforts to make and distribute hundreds of sandwiches for the homeless. They received well-deserved acclaim on television's *60 Minutes.*

Then I must tell you about a "freeway Good Samaritan" I just heard about. One of the nicest and most talented persons I know had a traumatic blowout on her way to our church, where she serves as worship leader. Cars whizzed by at their customary breakneck speeds. Many rubbernecked, but none stopped. That is, until a certain man pulled up. With a big smile, he got out of his car and offered to help.

He inconvenienced himself that morning. He helped change the tire, even though considerable time was required and the grease took its toll on his clothes.

Upon his completion of the task, my friend thanked him profusely. His reaction: "I'm the one who receives the blessing."

As he drove off, my relieved friend couldn't help noticing his license plate. It read "LVG 2B KD" (living to be kind).

So the point has been established that compassion must be seen as an offensive, rather than simply a defensive, strategy. It charges rather than barricades. As one writer states it, compassion must be "dressed up in work clothes and sent out onto the streets [and freeways] of men and women."

But before we can be truly compassionate, it's imperative that we comprehend what it is. Let's lean forward to have a closer look.

Reaching Out to Touch

A dictionary of theology defines compassion as "love's emotional response to actual distress or some impending calamity in the life of another."[2] The term is derived from the Latin words that together mean "to suf-

2. W. Stephen Gunter, "Compassion," in *Beacon Dictionary of Theology*, ed. Richard S. Taylor (Kansas City: Beacon Hill Press of Kansas City, 1983), 127.

fer with." Thus, to be compassionate means to enter the arena of pain, to share in brokenness and anguish, to cry out with those in misery.[3]

In the New Testament the Greek word most commonly used is *splangknon*, which suggests feeling great pity, close identification with, and intense feeling. Its literal meaning is "being moved in one's innermost being."[4]

God's compassion results from the infinite greatness of His love. Seeing the misery of creation, the Creator conspicuously displayed His empathy in the gift of His Son (John 3:16).

And Jesus is our Heavenly Father's embodiment of compassion. He felt it toward a widow as her only son's draped casket passed by (Luke 7:12-13). He felt it toward the "harassed and helpless" crowds who followed Him "like sheep without a shepherd" (Matt. 9:36; 14:14). He felt it toward the 4,000 who had not eaten for three days (Mark 8:2) and toward two blind men sitting beside the Jericho road (Matt. 20:30, 34).

His response in each of these situations was not forced. It flowed naturally from a heart that was perfectly attuned to His Father's will. Nor was it paternalistic—to satisfy a need to control, overpower, or impress. Finally, it was in no sense manipulative. Those He helped owed Him nothing. In gratitude and faith, many responded to His teachings afterward, but they made those decisions themselves. He exercised no semblance of mind control.

Jesus gave no-strings-attached, free, loving compassion. And it was straight from the deepest recesses of His sinless, God-aligned heart. That required courage.

Furthermore, His life and teachings broadcast a message to us loud and clear: The Christian way is in reality the way of compassion. To His disciples He declares,

The late Hubert Humphrey, former vice president of the United States, had a unique way of expressing himself. Speaking to a group of Christian men, he held up a long pencil and said, "Gentlemen, just as the eraser is only a very small part and is used only when a mistake is made, so compassion is called upon only when things get out of hand." His conclusion: "The main part of life is competition; only the eraser is compassion."

But that was Hubert Humphrey talking. Our biblical blueprint considers compassion to be much more than an eraser. It is that, too, all right, but much more.

—Donald P. McNeill, Douglas A. Morrison, and Henri J. M. Nouwen, *Compassion: A Reflection on the Christian Life* (Garden City, N.Y.: Image Books, 1966), 6.

---

3. Donald P. McNeill, Douglas A. Morrison, and Henri J. M. Nouwen, *Compassion: A Reflection on the Christian Life* (Garden City, N.Y.: Image Books, 1966), 6.

4. Vine, *Expository Dictionary of New Testament Words,* 218.

"Be merciful [compassionate], just as your Father is merciful" (Luke 6:36). This theme is vividly underscored in the parable of the prodigal son. Capture the beautiful picture of this dramatic homecoming: "While he was still a long way off, his father saw him and was filled with compassion for him; he ran to his son, threw his arms around him and kissed him" (15:20).

John speaks of our need for compassion when he states, "If anyone has material possessions and sees his brother in need but has no pity on him, how can the love of God be in him? Dear children, let us not love with words or tongue but with actions and in truth" (1 John 3:17-18).

In academic language, John is telling us that compassion is not an elective. It's a required course—absolutely necessary for graduating into heaven.

The first-century Church learned its lessons well. Here is how Aristides, an ancient philosopher, described it:

> Falsehood is not found among them; and they love one another, and from widows they do not turn away their esteem; and they deliver the orphan from him who treats him harshly. And he who has gives to him who has not, without boasting. And when they see a stranger, they take him into their homes and rejoice over him as a very brother; for they do not call them brethren after the flesh, but brethren after the spirit and in God. And whenever one of their poor passes from the world, each one of them according to his ability gives heed to him and carefully sees to his burial. And if they hear that one of their number is imprisoned or afflicted on account of the name of their Messiah, all of them anxiously minister to his necessity, and if it is possible to redeem him they set him free.
>
> And if there is among them any that is poor and needs, and if they have no spare food, they fast two or three days in order to supply the needy their lack of food.[5]

This is inspiring to contemplate and naturally leads us to ask, What evidences of compassion are we observing in the lives of our Christian brothers and sisters today?

Surprisingly, this New Testament virtue can pop up in some pretty unlikely people.

Meet a "Porcupine Care Bear"

My wife has a very compassionate friend. If you were around her for 10 minutes, however, you would probably conclude that she is anything but compassionate.

---

5. Robert E. Webber, *The Secular Saint* (Grand Rapids: Zondervan Publishing House, 1979), 84.

This gal exudes abrasiveness. Positive attitude? Norman Vincent Peale would probably turn from her and run. Winsomeness? No way. Her entire demeanor betrays her.

You get the picture. Many people consider her to be one super turn-off. That's why she's rarely invited to anyone's home.

And that's why my wife volleys snide comments when she is seen relating to her, comments such as "Why do you even bother talking to her?" and "You mean you're actually friends?" Does the lady pick up these rejection cues? There's no question about it. Down deep, she realizes that she has little chance of being accepted. And this really hurts her. As a result, she's abrasive to conceal her intense pain. Sure, it's a survival technique. But it's also a crying out for attention. In effect, she's saying, "Please recognize that I exist. I count for something, don't I?"

But don't close the book on her yet. Cease categorizing. Otherwise, you'll be mistaken.

My perceptive spouse has always seen this lady for what she is: one overactive "compassion dispenser." She gives from the heart—in a way in which people are not made to feel obligated. And she does so continuously, without fanfare, incognito.

Here are just some of her acts of compassion. She
- sits with sick hospital patients who have had surgery
- frequently writes notes of encouragement
- arranges large dinner parties in her home for the needy and elderly

Now, most people don't wish to get close enough to learn of her compassionate gestures. When they see her coming, all they want to do is to avoid her. Some have noticed her acts of compassion but quickly discount them. In their opinion, she cancels out any good works by being so hard to get along with. Such persons have not bothered to examine the underlying reasons for her behavior—nor tried to relate to her world.

I've given considerable thought to this entire scenario. It seems that there are some valuable lessons to learn:

1. *The lady's compassion is to be applauded. Nevertheless, it must be admitted that she undercuts its impact by continuing to behave offensively. How many of us fall into this same trap?*

As stated in *Walls or Bridges: How to Build Relationships That Glorify God*, we often inadvertently turn off others by being oblivious, obnoxious, or ostentatious.[6]

---

6. Jon Johnston, *Walls or Bridges: How to Build Relationships That Glorify God* (Grand Rapids: Baker Book House, 1988), 75.

We fail to remember that others often judge us by the visible manifestations of our personality. And when our observers are non-Christians, this judgment is frequently extended to other Christians—and even to the Lord we serve.

It behooves us to sandpaper, file, and buff the rough edges of our personalities and to forever reject the notion that "we are what we are and can never change."

2. *The elitist responses of her accusers don't seem to "cut New Testament pie." In fact, in God's eyes, they could be considered far worse than the abrasive lady.* To prejudge and cut someone off, as they have done, cannot be condoned. Such rejection is anathema to authentic discipleship. It is elitist, pure and simple.

I have this feeling that their rejection extends to far more than her "porcupine" personality. Essentially, they dislike her because they have concluded that she's basically inferior, unworthy, a loser.

And that's a reflection on them. Dan Reeves had it right when he stated, "You can tell the character of a man by the way he treats those who can do nothing for him."

But here's the tragedy of the situation: This lady has no possible way of overcoming their adverse judgment. Even the most compassionate actions on her part can never reverse their opinion or earn their respect. In their book, she's doomed because of what they perceive her to be.

> *⁓*
> The *Life Application Study Bible* lists these wrongs associated with favoritism—rejecting some people while embracing those considered elite:
>
> A. It is inconsistent with Christ's teachings.
> B. It results from evil thoughts.
> C. It belittles people made in God's image.
> D. It is a by-product of selfish motives.
> E. It goes against the biblical definition of love.
> F. It shows a lack of mercy to those less fortunate.
> G. It is hypocritical.
> H. It is sin.
>
> —*Life Application Study Bible*, s.v. "favoritism." Copyright © 1988, by Tyndale House Publishers, Inc., Wheaton, Illinois 60189. All rights reserved. Used by permission.

Under such conditions, I'm not certain how many of us would have her kind of courage. Our predominant reactions would likely be "What is the use?" "What do I have to gain?" "I might as well toss in the towel."

3. *Those who have continued to affirm this lady, like my wife, deserve credit. They've had to courageously overlook the elitists—who consider them "guilty by association."*

My father used to say that doing good while suffering criticism from "good" people is like "building the wagon and carrying the load at the same time."

It seems as if those who refuse to extend arms of love would refrain from attacking those who do. Perhaps being personally uninvolved may predispose them to such negative attitudes. Maybe in actuality they're simply being consistently uncompassionate!

Nevertheless, their actions are an increased burden on the shoulders of the compassionate—and a serious affront to our Savior, who embodies loving compassion.

Flipping Over the Coin

Granted, compassion is interwoven with Christian discipleship. Compassion is not optional—it's a necessity. To claim to be one of His and to portray a lack of compassion is serious business. Compassion requires true courage indeed.

Looking at the positive side of the coin, compassion gives luster and brilliance to our lives. It's the gateway to meaningful, significant living. Furthermore, it's but an outward overflow of Christ's Spirit, who reigns within. For that reason, it should come naturally when our lives are aligned with His will.

But don't get me wrong. The results of compassion are not always instantly apparent. Often there must be time for our compassion seeds to germinate. We must be patient as we anticipate the harvest.

Also, compassion always has a high price. It never comes easily, nor should we approach it with a cavalier attitude. In his inimitable style, C. S. Lewis explains:

> Love anything, and your heart will certainly be wrung and possibly broken. If you want to [keep] it intact, you must give your heart to no one. . . . Wrap it carefully around with hobbies and little luxuries, avoid all entanglements; lock it up safe in the casket . . . of your selfishness. But in that casket—safe, dark, motionless, airless—it will change. It will not be broken; it will become unbreakable, impenetrable, irredeemable. . . . The only place outside heaven where you can be perfectly safe from all the dangers . . . of love is hell.[7]

In spite of its risks, compassion is well worth the price.

He Had to Reach Up to Touch Bottom

Jesus said, "I tell you the truth, whatever you [do] for one of the least of these brothers of mine, you [do] for me" (Matt. 25:40).

Ted Stallard undoubtedly qualifies as "one of the least"—turned off by

---

7. Ibid., 63.

school, very sloppy in appearance, expressionless, unattractive. Even his teacher, Miss Thompson, enjoyed bearing down with her red pen as she placed Xs beside his many wrong answers.

If only she had studied his records more carefully. They read,

1st grade: Ted shows promise with his work and attitude but [has] poor home situation.

2nd grade: Ted could do better. Mother seriously ill. Receives little help from home.

3rd grade: Ted is good boy but too serious. He is a slow learner. His mother died this year.

4th grade: Ted is very slow but well behaved. His father shows no interest whatsoever.

Christmas arrived. The children piled elaborately wrapped gifts on their teacher's desk. Ted brought one too. It was wrapped in brown paper and held together with Scotch tape.

Miss Thompson opened each gift as the children crowded around to watch. Out of Ted's package fell a gaudy rhinestone bracelet, with half of the stones missing, and a bottle of cheap perfume.

The children began to snicker. But she silenced them by splashing some of the perfume on her wrist and letting them smell it. She put the bracelet on too.

At day's end, after the other children had left, Ted came by the teacher's desk and said, "Miss Thompson, you smell just like my mother. And the bracelet looks real pretty on you. I'm glad you like my presents." Then he left.

Miss Thompson got down on her knees and asked God to forgive her and to change her attitude.

The next day the children were greeted by a reformed teacher, one committed to loving each of them—especially the slow ones, and especially Ted.

Surprisingly—or maybe *not* surprisingly—Ted began to show great improvement. He actually caught up with most of the students and even passed a few.

Several years went by. Miss Thompson heard nothing from Ted for a long time. Then one day she received this note:

Dear Miss Thompson,

I wanted you to be the first to know.

I will be graduating second in my class.

Love,
Ted

Four years later, another note arrived:

Dear Miss Thompson,

They just told me I will be graduating first in my class. I wanted you to be the first to know.

The university has not been easy, but I liked it.

Love,
Ted

And four years later:

Dear Miss Thompson,

As of today, I am Theodore Stallard, M.D. How about that? I wanted you to be the first to know.

I am getting married next month, the 27th to be exact. I want you to come and sit where my mother would sit if she were alive. You are the only family I have now; Dad died last year.

Love,
Ted

Miss Thompson attended that wedding and sat where Ted's mother would have sat. The compassion she had shown that young man entitled her to that privilege.

Let's have some real courage and start giving to "one of the least." He may become a Ted Stallard. Even if that doesn't happen, we will have been faithful to the One who has always treated us—as unworthy as we are—like *very special people.*[8]

8. Swindoll, *Quest for Character,* 178-81. Copyright © 1982 by Charles R. Swindoll, Inc. Used by permission of Zondervan Publishing House.

9

RELINQUISHING THE SECURITY BLANKET
COURAGE IS RISK

Security is like the side of a swimming pool.
We can use it to cling to or to push off from.
—Terry Sullivan

Courage is grace under pressure.
—Ernest Hemingway

Leave the irreparable past in His hands,
and step out in the irresistible future with Him.
—Oswald Chambers

silver jet pierced the azure sky. Suddenly it reached a large mass of dark, billowing storm clouds. The aircraft was jolted from side to side. Drinks spilled. Babies started crying.

Let's pick up an actual conversation between author Tony Campolo and the nun who trembled beside him.

Tony: Sister, can I say something to calm you?

Nun: (No response—continuing in a state of panic)

Tony: Sister, you should remember that Jesus said, "I am with you always."

Nun: Oh, no He didn't! He said, "*Lo*, I am with you always"!

Have you ever been forced into a high-risk situation? I mean *really* high-risk—such as

- being told that you must have a life-threatening operation
- having to jump from one mountain cliff to another
- needing to enter a building that has just received a bomb threat

For most of us, risk taking is not our favorite pastime. It makes our hearts race. Our knuckles turn white. Our minds fill with worry. Usually we

95

take risks only when we see no other alternative—when we're boxed into a corner.

Safety and security are a top priority. That's why we buckle up, run to the medicine cabinet when scratched, and make certain that our drinking water is pure.

And that's why we avoid tackling formidable enemies. We would rather avoid bullies or flee from them. As one person put it, it's better to be a live coward than a dead hero. Another echoed the same sentiment: Sissies live longer.[1]

But though our natural inclinations pull us in the direction of security, we know a life of hypercaution is one of insignificance. Robert Louis Stevenson indicted the attitude of safety and prudence as "that dismal fungus."[2]

The truth is plain: More failure is the result of excess caution than of bold experimentation with new ideas. Without sufficient daring, our lives will become failures.

Ask any salesperson. Whenever he or she ventures forth to push a product, there's plenty of risk involved. People are guaranteed to say no often. But to those who continue risking, the results are rewarding. One study on people in sales revealed

48 percent make only one call on the same person, then quit.

25 percent make two calls, then cease.

15 percent make three calls, then desist.

12 percent make four or more calls—but they earn 80 percent of all profit.[3]

Allow me to stop and make a qualification. I'm not making an appeal for impulsive recklessness. Even for risk takers, preventive measures and logical thinking are musts. It's just that once we're convinced that we should act, we must not be tentative.

As a child, I recall Davy Crockett advising, "Be sure you're right—then go ahead." He did. I should have followed that advice more often.

Realizing the good that can come to us through risk taking, why do we remain tucked away in our nests of security?

---

1. Another more familiar way of stating this principle: "He who fights and runs away / Lives to fight another day."

2. J. Oswald Sanders, *Spiritual Leadership: A Timely and Practical Guide to Working Effectively with People* (Chicago: Moody Press, 1967), 117.

3. These figures were quoted in a sermon. No source was supplied. It is also popular knowledge that the typical salesman hears 40 noes to every 1 yes.

The Spoilers

According to one author, many of us have attitudes that paralyze our thinking and lock us up in "Status Quo Penitentiary." Here are the mental locks that keep us prisoners:

1. "Give the right answer."
2. "That's not logical."
3. "Follow the rules."
4. "Be practical."
5. "Avoid ambiguity."
6. "To err is wrong."
7. "Play is frivolous."
8. "That's not my area."
9. "Don't be foolish."
10. "I'm not creative."[4]

The same author says that nothing less than a "whack on the side of the head" can dislodge these mind-sets.

I advise a "whack on the heart." It seems that little else can change entrenched attitudes. How does this "whack on the heart" happen? What kinds of perspectives must be cultivated? And what's the sequence of developing these perspectives?

To begin with, we must explore the *origins* of our mental inhibitors. By understanding their sources, we'll discover clues that will help us disengage from these locked mind-sets. They essentially come from four sources, which can be thought of as the "frowning prison guards" who guard our cells.

    Source No. 1—Fear (When we're scared to death, we have little appetite for chance taking.)

    Source No. 2—Perfectionism (When it must always be done "correctly," we believe it's best not to risk failure.)

    Source No. 3—Laziness (When we lack energy, and slump back into atrophy, and "will to venture" dissipates.)

    Source No. 4—Traditionalism (To always "do it like our father did it" kills any risk taking.)[5]

When we buy into any of the above, we're consumed with a doubt that makes us unwilling to risk. Nevertheless, we can encourage ourselves with hope. God can cause the doubt to disappear and replace it with a desire to venture forth.

---

4. Roger von Oech, *A Whack on the Side of the Head* (New York: Warner Books, 1983), 9.

5. Swindoll, *Quest for Character*, 200. Copyright © 1982 by Charles R. Swindoll, Inc. Used by permission of Zondervan Publishing House.

These biblical heroes are cases in point. They triumphantly escaped their restricting doubts, and the *ventures* turned into victorious *adventures:*

Doubter	Doubtful Moment	Reference
Abraham	When God told him he would be a father in old age	Gen. 17:17
Sarah	When she heard she would be a mother in old age	Gen. 18:12
Moses	When God told him to return to Egypt to lead his people	Exod. 3:10-15
Israelites	Whenever they faced difficulties in the wilderness	Exod. 16:1-3
Gideon	When told he would help save Israel	Judg. 6:14-23
Zechariah	When told he would be a father in old age	Luke 1:18
Thomas	When told Jesus had risen from the dead	John 20:24-25[6]

These people of God, who became courageous venturers, started out as world-class doubters. But our Heavenly Father showed great patience with them. And His patience paid off.

Key point: Doubt is never a bad starting point *if* we're not content to remain there. Once we escape from the mental shackles and slip past these ever watchful guards, we are free to begin dreaming.

Many of us get bogged down with nagging problems and responsibilities. As a result, we remain mired in doubt. We neglect to dream.[7] And this is tragic. Why? Because little is ever accomplished that's not first envisioned. The writer of Proverbs puts it even more strongly: "Where there is no vision, the people perish" (29:18, KJV).

Dreaming and vision, though commendable, are still not enough for those of us who follow the Man from Galilee. They weren't for Him. They're not for us.

You see, Jesus was much more than a visionary—He was a missionary! The difference lies in the nature of the dreaming.

---

6. *Life Application Study Bible,* s.v. "doubt." Copyright © 1988, by Tyndale House Publishers, Inc., Wheaton, Illinois 60189. All rights reserved. Used by permission.

7. See Harold Ivan Smith, *No Fear of Trying: Turn Your "I've Always Wanted To" Wishes into Reality* (Nashville: Thomas Nelson Publishers, 1988).

Not Just Any Dream Will Do

Tyrants and unethical businessmen dream. So do murderers and thieves. I'm reminded of how the Birdman of Alcatraz was obsessed by his dream of escape, how Alexander the Great was consumed by his dream of conquest, how J. Paul Getty was driven by his desire to acquire wealth.

But we're different. As with Jesus, our aspirations must go through the litmus test of God's Word. Scripture accurately distinguishes between good and bad dreams.

And what's a good dream, according to the Bible? Allow me to paraphrase the words of Paul in Phil. 4:8: Whatever is *true*, whatever is *noble*, whatever is *right*, whatever is *pure*, whatever is *lovely*, whatever is *admirable* —we will *dream* on those things.

Elsewhere Paul declares, "Since, then, you have been raised with Christ, set your hearts on *things above* . . . not on earthly things" (Col. 3:1-2, emphasis added).

The dreams of non-Christians stand in radical contrast to truth, rightness, purity, and the other spiritual qualities listed above. Instead, according to the apostle, they're likely to dream on things such as "sexual immorality, impurity, lust, evil desires and greed, which is idolatry" (v. 5). Their focus is on pleasing themselves rather than God or others; "lay[ing] up . . . treasures upon earth" rather than "in heaven" (Matt. 6:19-20, KJV); and climbing to the top of the ladder—even if it means pushing others off as they ascend.

Perhaps it's the perspective that keeps non-Christians from understanding what motivates Christians to risk for the right. To non-Christians, it all seems incredibly foolish. They simply fail to see the value of the Christians' kind of dream.

Not long ago I heard a story that illustrates this incongruity more than any I've ever heard. Let me share it.

A Clash of Dreams

A minister friend of mine in San Diego celebrated his son's 21st birthday by taking him on a harbor cruise. The ship was *The Invader*, custom-made in Quincy, Massachusetts, in 1905 for William Borden, founder of the milk company by that name.

The ship's captain explained that there were no heirs to assume ownership of the boat; thus, it was sold at public auction and ended up in San Diego.

In the week following the cruise, Pastor Paul heard the rest of the story and just had to share it with his congregation the next Sunday morning. I visited his service that day and will never forget the story's impact on my own life.

The Bordens had a son who was given every advantage imaginable throughout his youth. Frequently, they reminded him that he was the person chosen to inherit the company and that he should begin grooming himself for the awesome responsibility.

Then one day off to college he went. While there, some friends introduced him to Jesus Christ. That's when *everything* changed, especially his dreams! He announced to his father that he would be relinquishing his future in the company to become a missionary to the Far East.

The parents' shock was almost too much to bear. *What? Give up what most Americans dream about—power, status, wealth, possessions, including the luxurious family yacht? How ungrateful! How tragic! How incomprehensible!*

Mr. Borden scrambled to do all within his power to talk his son out of his "foolish" decision. He offered further enticements. He attempted to induce guilt. He even tried scare tactics, warning his son of a plague that was spreading through the Far East. But it was all to no avail. The young man's mind was made up—he would follow God's dream for his life.

And so he departed.

After a few months, William Sr. received a letter from the missionary board. As he opened it, he thought, "Has my son been honored in a special way? Better yet, are they informing me that he's coming home for good?"

Then, as he began reading, tears welled up in his eyes. His son had died—he had contracted the fatal disease.

Mr. Borden's intense sorrow soon turned to anger as he thought about the "what might have been." If only . . . if only . . .

The funeral came and went, but the sorrow remained. In fact, it intensified. Then, some months later a small package arrived in the mail. It was from another missionary who had been the son's close friend. The letter inside spoke of their friendship and the son's tremendous ministry. It concluded with this postscript: "Mr. Borden, you will find your son's Bible enclosed. It meant so much to him, and I know it will to you."

The milk magnate began to thumb through the Book he knew very little about. Then, just as he was about to close it, he noticed some words scratched on the back flyleaf. The date beside corresponded to the week before his son's death.

Upon closer inspection, he discovered that this was his son's own handwriting. His heart was overwhelmed, as he slowly and softly read to himself:

NO RESERVE
NO RETREAT
NO REGRET

The words were like sharp knives that punctured his calloused heart. Yet those words caused Mr. Borden to begin rethinking his priorities.

His son had a dream—a dream with eternal significance. In following that dream, he had risked everything. But, in so doing, what he gained was infinitely immeasurable.

William Borden realized this now. Although he still grieved, he no longer grieved with resentment. Rather, his grief was tinged with deep respect.

An inspiring story indeed. But many of us no doubt see William Borden Jr.'s dream as beyond our comprehension. We assume that this guy was some sort of a saint, a one-in-a-million person not at all like the rest of us. We're not Borden heirs by a long shot—we're doing well just to keep milk on our tables!

Is there a way we can bring this business of risk down to where we live? I believe there is.

Our Nine-to-Five World

We must realize that risking for Jesus is a biblical assignment for all believers—whether we live in a mansion or a shanty, whether we eat lobster three times a week or dine with the same frequency on beans and corn bread.

If we're truly Christians, we'll risk. The Lord is counting on us. And the advancement of His kingdom on earth is at stake. H. W. K. Moule said, "The frontiers of the kingdom of God were never advanced by men and women of caution."

Furthermore, our abandonment of security will be rewarded. Jesus said so: "Everyone who has left houses or brothers or sisters or father or mother or children or fields for my sake will receive a hundred times as much and will inherit eternal life" (Matt. 19:29). We must begin to courageously risk *where* we are, *as* we are.

In what ways can we begin to risk? Here are a few suggestions:

- Dare to invite another to accept Jesus as his or her Savior; Prov. 11:30 declares, "He who wins souls is wise."
- Put ourselves in environments where we're likely to be ridiculed for our faith (for example, refusing to drink alcohol when everyone else is).
- Get to know someone whom others consider a real "turnoff" or "loser."
- Lovingly confront someone who is unintentionally hurting another.

- Take on a high-risk project that's guaranteed to yield little public acclaim and take its toll on your patience—something others feel is too far beneath them to undertake.

No doubt, each of us has other suggestions tailored to our own situations.

We know when we're playing it safe and opting for our own security and comfort. And deep down, we know when and how we should stand up and be counted. I have to believe that because of an incident in my own life. Allow me to share it with you.

God's Office of Career Placement

Those of you who know me pretty well might imagine someone saying to me, "Boy, Jon, you're pretty safe. You teach at that big, fancy university out west—and you're not encumbered by any denominational supervision or restriction."

Someone else might say, "Jon, you'll certainly never have to worry about your career. You can say or do anything you want."

To be honest, a part of me believed this—until one particular incident in the late 1980s. That's when it was pointed out to me by leaders in my denomination that my career was in jeopardy—unless I shut up fast. You see, there was a little problem with the leadership in my local church.

People are still telling me that I kept my head in the sand too long, because I didn't speak out sooner. I just didn't want to believe what was happening. Was I ever naive!

Well, the Lord cleared it really fast in my mind—with some rather shocking evidence. And He told me that I would have to join in with those who were taking a stand.

I never questioned His voice, but like David of old, I seriously wondered if He had asked the right person.

I said, "Lord, this is a tough assignment. Can't You just take care of it yourself?"

He said to me, "I'm counting on you, and I'll be with you each step of the way."

So I decided to contact one of our denominational leaders. After I explained the situation, he responded, "That's all well and good. We do need to do what's right. But, Jon, it seems that you're up on the ladder—you've earned a measure of respect in our denomination."

I looked shocked and replied, "I hadn't really given that much thought."

He replied, "Let me put it to you straight—if you stand up on this issue, I fear for your career."

We parted. And I passed off what he had said.

I had no option but to go all the way to the top—which meant flying out to talk with someone higher up. When I finished my presentation there, this man looked me straight in the eyes—in front of another board member—and said, "Jon, you know you're pretty much up there on the ladder."

"What exactly do you mean?" I asked.

He replied, "I mean that you could seriously harm your career."

I could take no more and said, "If you've read my books, you know that my career is far less important to me than doing what the Lord asks me to do." He nodded.

Well, you're probably wondering what finally happened. To abbreviate this story, let me tell you that the whole situation was resolved. Our church was freed from the shadow of suspicion, deception, and intimidation. And with new leadership, after just one year, it registered at least a 33 percent growth in every area.

Still, I'm quite sure that in the minds of some, my "respect, power, and recognition" were damaged. But is that what really matters? Who cares about my career? Besides, after I said yes to Christ's assignment, it was not *my* career any longer.

Paraphrasing Mother Teresa, former senator Mark Hatfield once said to our faculty, "It's not how *successful* we are, in the world or in the church's eye, but how *faithful* we are to the principles we know to be right."

10

$\mathcal{I}$N THE $\mathcal{S}$AME $\mathcal{B}$UILDING BUT ON $\mathcal{A}$NOTHER $\mathcal{F}$LOOR

COURAGE IS SOLITUDE

Many of us, resolving to be courageous, resemble the mosquito who found himself in a nudist colony. He knew what to do— he just couldn't decide where to start!

Courage is almost a contradiction in terms. It means a strong desire to live taking the form of a readiness to die.
—G. K. Chesterton

People whose character is being developed, stretched, and deepened aren't hesitant to say "Go," even though the majority say "No."
—Charles Swindoll

$\mathcal{M}$rs. Carlo Ponti—does that name ring a bell? You may know her better as Sophia Loren—world-renowned star of over 100 films.

I had heard about her moving to southern California and her son, Carlo Ponti Jr., enrolling in our university. One day he dropped by my office to sign up for our China trip. His father, famous producer of such films as *Doctor Zhivago*, accompanied him. They were very cordial and easy to talk with.

Before leaving my office, they asked if my wife and I might possibly agree to come to their house for dinner. Sophia wanted to meet the people who would be taking her son halfway around the world. Excited about the prospect but trying to look composed, I assured them that we could probably manage to work it into our schedule.

The next week I was doing some work at my office when the phone rang. It was Sophia herself calling to confirm a time. Her voice was warm as she furnished the directions.

On the appointed evening we drove to the Ponti estate. We were welcomed at the front door by the maid, who invited us to be seated in the liv-

ing room. We were impressed by the simple elegance of the decor. Carlo
Ponti Sr. and his son came in. They were both friendly, and we laughed at
stories about their dog, snacked on hors d'oeuvres, and discussed our plans
for the upcoming trip.

Then Sophia entered. She was as beautiful as you might imagine, and
we instantly found her personality to be equally as attractive. She was an
excellent conversationalist, passing off any references to her many success-
es and expressing an interest in our lives.

Before long, we were eating dinner at a marble table that overlooked a
beautiful garden. The dinner lasted three hours, though it seemed like only
10 minutes or so. Carlo and Sophia teased each other. They asked questions about our university, the state of affairs in China, and a host of other
things—such as the feasibility of using tapes while asleep to improve self-
confidence. Concerning the latter, I recall suggesting the reading of Scripture instead.

Sophia told about her mother in Italy, whom she said she telephoned
every day. Then she described her other son, who was attending school in
Switzerland.

There was no name-dropping, no put-downs, no showbiz talk, no
bragging about achievements or awards—just good old-fashioned conversation about things we're all interested in: family, values, humorous moments
of embarrassment, and so on. Through it all, Sophia was the perfect hostess, constantly making sure that we were enjoying our food.

The time came to depart. Sophia walked with us to the front room,
where she autographed two or three of her books. She quietly handed them
to my wife, Cherry. We said our good-byes and went out the front door.
Our gracious hostess stood and watched us as we descended the steps to
our car. When we looked back, she waved.

The trip to China went very well. And I was not surprised to observe
that Carlo Jr. was a perfect gentleman throughout. It was very evident that
his caring parents had instilled worthwhile principles in his life.

Of course, after our close contact, I was very interested to read Sophia
Loren's autobiography—a story of challenge and courage in difficult cir-
cumstances.

More than Meets the Eye

Sophia was born in Pozzuoli, Italy. Her father abandoned the family,
and she grew up an impoverished slum urchin. At school, she was merci-
lessly teased about her illegitimacy.

Then, Nazi soldiers invaded her town. They stole from the people and drew attacks from Allied troops. In one bombing raid, Sophia was hit by shrapnel. When the war started going badly for Germany, she witnessed the Nazi soldiers killing her neighbors.

After the war, Sophia's personal war continued. She tried learning to play the piano but quit because her mother banged her over the head when she made mistakes. Overcoming all the obstacles, she managed to break into films.

She met, and lived with, Carlo—who was older than she—and whom she considered security giver, father image, and lover. The Vatican denounced her as a "public sinner," because Ponti was married at the time.

Finally, after his divorce, they were married. Trials continued—including a series of miscarriages, a robbery, and finally, a mix-up in taxes that led to the Italian government issuing a warrant for Sophia's arrest.

In spite of her difficulties, Sophia continued to make films and to impress the world with her beauty and talent. In time, she and Carlo had two healthy sons and moved to America.

At this point in the book, I surmised that all the bad times were behind her. Sophia could now take a well-deserved deep breath and truly enjoy life.

Well, life isn't like that for the famous. They never escape the penetrating public eye and can never disregard the possibility of some deranged killer stalking their path. In short, they must isolate themselves. The result: loneliness.

Toward the end of the book, Carlo Ponti Sr. describes his wife as "antisocial." There could be no spur-of-the-moment dinners in a nearby restaurant or a night on the town. Why? "The moment we put our feet out of the [house], we are molested by the public. . . . When we go out, we are curiosities. The press assaults us and outrageously distorts what they write about us."

He goes on, "We mostly avoid parties, because if we go to one person's house, then others are miffed if we don't go to theirs."

He concludes, "Some feel that Sophia does not have fun, is not enjoying her life, because she stays home so much. But they don't realize what an ordeal it is when she does go out."

Then he writes these telling words: *She is a prisoner when she goes out, and free to be herself only when she's behind her own four walls.*[1]

---

1. A. E. Hotchner, *Sophia Living and Loving: Her Own Story* (New York: William Morrow and Co., 1979), 224.

The Flip Side of Fame

What's true about Sophia Loren is true for all who distinguish themselves from the masses. They simply stand out. They're visible.

We see this especially in the lives of the former presidents of the United States. As one writer declared, "Loneliness stalks where the buck stops."

Consider President Abraham Lincoln. Today we're convinced of his greatness, but on the day he died, Lincoln's critics were numerous and fierce. He endured a lonely agony that reflected our country's turmoil — just after being ripped to shreds by a cruel and costly civil war.

On the night he was assassinated, at Ford Theatre in Washington, D.C., these items were removed from Lincoln's pockets:

- a handkerchief embroidered with "A. Lincoln"
- a farm boy's pocketknife
- a purse containing a $5 Confederate bill
- a spectacles case held together by a string
- some old, worn newspaper clippings

The clippings told of his great deeds. One reported a speech by John Bright, which said Lincoln is "one of the greatest men of all times." It seems touchingly pathetic that this "man for the ages" had to seek self-assurance from a few old newspaper clippings. See him as he reads them under the candle's flickering flame — all alone — in the Oval Office.[2] He's the picture of loneliness.

This type of loneliness is also true of sports personalities. When they perform well, they're considered heroes. But when they're in a slump, the "boo birds" come out. Suddenly those who received cheers only a few days before experience the intense loneliness that accompanies rejection.

In addition to loneliness are the threats. When former Los Angeles Dodger pitcher Joe Moeller spoke to my community organization class, he said players constantly receive threatening phone calls and death threats from "sickies." Menacing voices say things like "Don't plan on playing another game after tonight. There will be a gun pointed at your temple in the third inning."

The point is clear: To become *visible* in the public eye is to become *vulnerable*. You become vulnerable to abuse, vulnerable to attack, vulnerable to invasion of privacy — and as a result, vulnerable to the pangs of loneliness.

Facing the world with that extreme kind of vulnerability requires great courage.

---

2. Swindoll, *Quest for Character*, 62. Copyright © 1982 by Charles R. Swindoll, Inc. Used by permission of Zondervan Publishing House.

A Timeless Principle

This reality is not confined to today. It has existed since humanity began singling out individuals for special attention.

One sociologist refers to such individuals as "marginal." They seem to be at best bigger than life, and at worst they appear abnormal. Somehow they elude categories.[3]

When these people become famous, we term them "celebrities." When they're perceived as infamous, we call them "deviants." In either case, they simply don't fit in with others, like brown shoes with a black tuxedo. As a result, they're treated differently, so differently that they often feel compelled to retreat into the safety and serenity of their own solitude.

When persons become visible or "poke their heads above the crowd," they're singled out for special attention—so much so that they're forced to *isolate* or *insulate* themselves. When that occurs, intense loneliness is the result.

What does this have to do with courage? Simply this: Many around us hesitate to take courageous stands. They take the way of least resistance. If they do take a stand, their courage relates to an area of little consequence —a tempest in a teapot—or they stand firm in an area that concerns self-gratification.

When we, as followers of Jesus, are courageous on issues that really count, we set ourselves apart like speckled birds in a single-color flock. We're perceived as nonconformists. People notice that we're not marching in lockstep to this world's drummer, and often it bugs them. Try not swearing around those who do. Or refusing an alcoholic beverage when others are imbibing. Or not laughing at a smutty story or ethnic joke.

In a more positive way, visibly interact with people whom others consider to be "pure trash" or "hopeless." Express the need for compassion for those who are afflicted with AIDS. Bow your head to say grace before a meal.

All of these actions prompt others to think of us as special, different, or just plain weird. We'll stand out in their minds and be plopped into a category they title "other." Once categorized in this manner, we can be sure of being treated differently. Perhaps some people will show greater respect. But many, because of guilt, fear, or pure discomfort, will dispense varying degrees of ostracism. This will show itself through silence, stares, snide comments, and the like.

---

3. See Everett V. Stonequist, *The Marginal Man* (New York: Charles Scribner's Sons, 1937).

How are we likely to feel? Pretty lonely. We'll feel cut off—as if we're traveling our own road. We'll not be sure of being understood—even by other Christians or our families. We won't know if we're truly *liked* or if we're merely being *tolerated*.

Are there instances of courageous Christian personalities who were subject to these sentiments? Let's consider a few. Perhaps they'll help us to be better able to cope with our loneliness.

They Carried the Torch—Lighted

Courageous biblical leaders remained faithful throughout their solitude.

Moses was alone on the mount and alone in the plain. He experienced the crushing loneliness of misunderstanding, unfair criticism, and questioning of motive. He had no close chums—no real confidants.

The prophets were the loneliest of men. *Enoch* walked alone in a decadent society as he proclaimed impending judgment. So did Elijah, Isaiah, Amos, and Hosea.

Hear *Jeremiah* as he says, "Alas, my mother, that you gave me birth, a man with whom the whole land strives and contends! I have neither lent nor borrowed, yet everyone curses me" (15:10).

Who could have experienced pangs of loneliness more than *Jonah*? He courageously proclaimed the message of imminent judgment to a heathen city of a million persons. But prior to this, it was not exactly "party time" in the stomach of that big fish.

Daniel stood tall. After being threatened with death for worshiping God, he intentionally prayed aloud through an open window. His enemies heard, tattled, and rejoiced as he was taken to the lions' den. Feel marginal? No loneliness we experience today could compare with what he must have felt as he stared at the bicuspids of those beasts.

We know that *David* had a remarkable friendship with Jonathan—but only in his early years. When he became Israel's king, his greatest battles, deepest prayers, and hardest decisions had to be made in solitude.

Then there is the gregarious *Paul*, who experienced the bitterness of being misunderstood by contemporaries, misrepresented by his enemies, and deserted by his converts and friends. Catch the pathos of his voice as he declares to Timothy, "You know that everyone in the province of Asia has deserted me" (2 Tim. 1:15).[4]

---

4. Sanders, *Spiritual Leadership*, 107-8.

Moving to more contemporary times, let's eavesdrop on retiring missionary Hudson Taylor as he explains the China Inland Mission assignment to his successor, *Dixon Hoste*. We see Hoste's somber countenance as the weight of responsibility is unloaded onto his shoulders. He wonders, "Can one man be courageous enough to carry this load?" The important meeting draws to a close. Those standing nearby hear Hoste's final words as he leaves Taylor's presence: "And now I have no one, no one but God!"

A. W. Tozer puts it straight: "Most of the world's great souls have been lonely. Loneliness seems to be the price a saint must pay for his saintliness."[5]

The bottom line is this: Today's courageous Christian must be someone who, while welcoming friendship and support of all who offer, has sufficient inner resources to stand alone—even to face fierce opposition—in obeying the Lord.

F. W. H. Meyers puts these sentiments in verse:

> *On without cheer of sister or of daughter,*
> *Yes, without stay of father or of son,*
> *Lone on the land, and homeless on the water,*
> *Pass I in patience till my work be done.*[6]

If loneliness is inevitable for those of us who choose to be courageous, we must have certain attitudes to help us cope. Let's examine some of these.

S.O.S. Kit for Lonely Stalwarts

Attitudes, defined by sociologists as our "learned inclinations to respond," can be powerful.

Situations that are perceived as negative and even hopeless by most can be perceived as springboards to opportunity. It's the old "Let's turn our lemons into lemonade" idea—and it works, especially as applied to that kind of loneliness that results from taking courageous stands.

What attitudes should be tucked away in our survival kit? Take a look at these, master them, and draw from them often:

1. *We must always remember that ours is a chosen loneliness.*

Many are lonely simply because they allow themselves to be "processed" by our impersonal, automated society. Switchboards, traffic jams, mass media, computers, junk mail, E-mail, and a host of other things that are encountered daily can take their toll. People begin to feel overpowered—like a cog in society's wheel.

---

5. Ibid., 108.
6. J. Oswald Sanders, *Spiritual Leaders: A Timely and Practical Guide to Working with People* (Chicago: Moody Press, 1967), 108. Used by permission.

But our loneliness comes because we've chosen to take courageous stands. Thus, we willfully say yes to the lonely pathway, not because we're victimized, but rather because we wish to be victors!

That thought should help us to stand taller and feel better.

2. *We must accept our loneliness without "excess baggage."*

Once we gain ascendancy over being depressed about our loneliness, there's the ever present temptation to allow it to collect additional attitudinal weight. Let me explain.

We can accept our loneliness but permit it to make us increasingly bitter or resentful. It becomes a "badge" to remind ourselves how bad we have it. And we have frequent "black-tie pity parties."

Also, our solitude can be attached to an attitude of self-righteousness. We can feel that our "cross" qualifies us for heavenly (and even earthly) VIP status.

These attitudes must be soundly rejected. Instead, we must bear our loneliness with quiet dignity—just as our Savior did when He stood accused before Pilate.

3. *As our courage is God's gift, so our loneliness is borne by His grace.*

We must remember that though we may be lonely, we're never really alone. The Lord is always with us.

Separated from the clamoring voices of others, we're better able to hear His voice. Without needing to conform to the demands of others, we're better able to follow His will. Our intimacy with Him can be accentuated because, in reality, it's just us and our Maker.

Charles Swindoll employs just the right words: "It is in lonely solitude that God delivers His best thoughts."[7]

Undeniably, our human nature craves company. It's only natural to want to share with others. To be in solitude is discomforting, especially for the Christian. But our loneliness need not hamstring us. With the attitudes above, we'll emerge victorious. And what appears to others to be an impediment can actually become a source of strength.

Just as the ground that lies fallow enriches itself for the next planting, so our solitude can be a period of spiritual nourishment—readying us for a future challenge.

Again, it comes down to the matter of attitudes we choose to embrace. Unfortunately, some have selected negative attitudes and have succumbed. Though tragic, their stories can teach us important lessons.

---

7. Swindoll, *Quest for Character*, 63. Copyright © 1982 by Charles R. Swindoll, Inc. Used by permission of Zondervan Publishing House.

The Dark Clouds Gathered

Few stories have made me sadder than that of Bob Pierce, founder of World Vision International. Most of us know this organization to be easily one of the largest Christian relief efforts to third world countries. Much of the World Vision success is due to Bob's wise leadership.

At the time of its inception, there were no other programs of its kind. Skeptics, inside and outside the church, doubted its value. And they let Bob Pierce know of their misgivings.

But Bob was a special person. His courage was unbelievable. He was a man of prayer, faith, and action. Once he was convinced that World Vision was God's will, there was no stopping him.

Many closed doors had to be pushed open. Money-raising was resented by some church leaders—viewed as "taking money from the church." Efforts to improve the quality of life (by digging wells or planting crops) were seen as unworthy. Some felt that Christians should only be preaching to these people.

Bob felt the impact of the criticism and questions, but he just kept marching forward. And it was a very lonely march.

In a radio interview, his daughter stated that he became "married to his job." He was gone weeks, even months, at a time. As a result, he became a stranger in his own home.

Then one of Bob's children committed suicide. His wife reached her limit of the pressures in the marriage. She and Bob separated.

It became evident that Bob was steadily sinking under the stress in his life and work. He even had a strong disagreement with his own board and resigned.

What a sorrowful picture! Here is the man who had courageously launched a great Christian organization. He had won hundreds, perhaps thousands, of souls to the Lord. Even the leaders of the third world countries respected him. Yet now we visualize him as an extremely lonely man —at a time in his life when he should have been inundated with friends and intimately involved with his family.

It's not for us to know or judge the causes of Bob's difficulties. Yes, he achieved many accomplishments for God's kingdom, but somewhere along the line, this great leader lost his perspective.

Courage? He had an inordinate quantity, and he pushed back many of Satan's frontiers. But unlike Moses and David, when the inevitable loneliness came to him, he was unable to cope. He walled himself in, developed unhealthy attitudes, saw his "empire" collapse and his family fragment.

Bob Pierce did gain a measure of serenity before his death. In fact, the

family had a brief reunion. It's also evident that the work he started continues in grand fashion.

Thus, his was not a wasted life—just one that was extremely lonely. And somehow he was unable to effectively cope within the confines of that solitude.

May we learn from his mistakes and accept our loneliness with pa-tience and even thanksgiving. Like Noah, let's courageously continue "building the boat," even though we're doing it ourselves and others don't seem to understand.

$\mathcal{G}$OING TO THE $\mathcal{M}$AT
COURAGE IS COMMITMENT

No problem facing our nation is so awesome, so complicated or so fraught with danger that the average citizen can't run away from it.
—Charlie Brown in a "Peanuts" comic strip episode

Whatever you can do, or dream you can, begin it.
Boldness has genius, power, and magic in it.
—Goethe

If the trumpet does not sound a clear call, who will get ready for battle?
—1 Cor. 14:8

$\mathcal{I}$ recently heard a tongue-in-cheek speech to graduating college seniors that highlighted the contrast between cushy college life and the harsh world of employment. It was titled "Ten Reasons Not to Get a Job." Some of those reasons mentioned were

- Your social life will be in shambles, because you'll need to get to bed at a decent hour.
- A job will prevent you from getting up late, watching favorite daytime soaps, and taking those long afternoon naps.
- Aware of your earning potential, your parents will charge you rent to live in your room, and your alumni association and church will expect generous offerings.
- Unlike college, you'll have no excused absences, free days to go to the beach, or permission to sleep through sessions.
- Worst of all, if you get a job, most likely, *you'll have to go to work.*[1]

Working at a job requires commitment—as does getting married, joining the armed services, taking care of a hamster, keeping up an automobile, and (let me add) pursuing a college career.

---

1. Presented by Nancy Magnussum-Fagan at a breakfast to graduating seniors. Taken from "Ten Reasons Not to Get a Job," in *The Harvard Lampoon Big Book of College Life*, ed. Steven G. Crist and George Meyer (Garden City, N.Y.: Doubleday, 1978).

Commitment is closely intertwined with courage. It implies courage to take on a challenge, courage to plow through obstacles along the way. It includes courage to back off when time and experience have proven such commitments unwise.

The dictionary defines commitment as "pledging oneself to a thing, idea, or person."[2] I like Lewis Smedes's definition better: "learning to live the love we promise."[3]

Commitment carries with it the idea of giving time, energy, and other resources in a total, hands-down manner. Mere involvement, by contrast, is less intense and sacrificial. As someone aptly put it, "A chicken was *involved* in my breakfast. She simply laid the egg. But a pig was truly *committed*—he furnished the bacon."

What are the results of being really committed? Let's begin by spotlighting the secular world.

The Gateway to Significance

A number of corporate managers in a study were asked if they voiced positions that (1) focused on the good of the company rather than personal benefit and (2) jeopardized their own careers.

Emerging from this study were the four leader types who are found in all organizations.

Type 1—courageous. These people express ideas to help the company improve in spite of personal risk or opposition.

Type 2—confronting. These people speak up, but only because of a personal vendetta against the company.

Type 3—calloused. These people neither know nor care whether they can do anything for the company; they feel helpless and hopeless, so they keep quiet.

Type 4—conforming. These people also remain quiet, but only because they loathe confrontation and love approval.[4]

The researchers discovered that the courageous managers accomplished the most, reported the highest job satisfaction, and eventually were commended by superiors. The commitment had certainly improved the quality of their lives.

Commitment always pays off. Why? Because it causes us to initiate,

---

2. *Random House Dictionary,* s.v. "commitment."

3. Lewis B. Smedes, *Caring and Commitment: Learning to Live the Love We Promise* (San Francisco: Harper and Row, 1988).

4. Harvey A. Hornstein, "When Corporate Courage Counts: During Hard Times, Business Is in Special Need of Lionhearted Management," *Psychology Today,* September 1986, 56, 58-60.

rather than to passively await, what happens. Commitment jump-starts our lives!

W. H. Murray put it very well:

Until one is committed, there is hesitancy, the chance to draw back, always ineffectiveness. Concerning all acts of initiative (and creation), there is one elementary truth, the ignorance of which kills countless ideas and splendid plans: that *the moment one definitely commits oneself, then providence moves too.*

All sorts of things occur to help one that would never otherwise have occurred. A whole stream of events issues from the decisions, raising in one's favor all manner of unforeseen incidents and meetings and material assistance, which no man would have dreamt would have come his way.[5]

This is illustrated in a story shared by radio commentator Earl Nightingale. A psychiatrist interviewed a number of skilled mountain climbers just prior to their attempts to climb Mount Everest, asking each, "Will you get to the top?"

The psychiatrist received a variety of responses, such as "We'll have to wait and see." "I'm going to give it my best shot." "I just hope I'm lucky."

But one man of slight build had a totally different answer. He softly but emphatically responded, *"Yes, I will."*

Not surprisingly, he was the first to make it to the peak. "Yes, I will"—three of the most potent words in our language. They're words of commitment, words that make possibilities realities. And these are words usually spoken through the lips of truly courageous persons.

But for the Christian, the commitments we make are much more praiseworthy than the kinds made by businesspeople and mountain climbers. Our focus rises far above monetary profit and personal achievement. Furthermore, our commitment requires much greater courage.

Primarily, we commit ourselves to a *Person,* to *people,* and to crucial *principles.* Let's closely examine each area.

Commitment to Christ, Our Highest Purpose

As previously mentioned, commitment to Jesus means taking on His identity. (See Gal. 2:20.) Ironically, after doing so, we become our true selves—with self-concepts that are healthy as well as holy.

I'll be a little more specific. There is what Augustine has termed a

---

5. This quote by W. H. Murray is from an uncirculated sheet of paper I found. No source was indicated.

"God-shaped void" in all of us. This empty space can be filled only by Christ's presence.

Francis A. Schaeffer explains it this way:

> It is impossible even to begin living the Christian life, or to know anything of true spirituality, before one is a Christian, and the only way to become a Christian is neither by trying . . . nor by hoping, but rather by *accepting Christ as Savior.* No matter how complicated, educated, or sophisticated we may be, or how simple we may be, we must come the same way. . . . This is true for all men, everywhere, through all space and all time. There are no exceptions. Jesus said a totally exclusive word: "No man cometh unto the Father, but by me" (John 14:6 [KJV]).[6]

Two Greek verbs for "repent" are used in the New Testament. Both pertain to sin. The first, *metamelonai,* connotes regret, remorse, or sorrow for past wrong (see Matt. 21:29; 2 Cor. 7:10). The second, *metanoeo,* implies a change of mind or purpose—a change that's always for the better: a turning from sin and a turning to God. In short, an about-face!

—W. E. Vine, *An Expository Dictionary of New Testament Words* (Old Tappan, N.J.: Fleming H. Revell Co., 1966), 279-80.

Be assured, Jesus Christ will never impose His will on ours. He quietly stands at the door of our hearts and knocks. (See Rev. 3:20.) It's up to us to open and ask Him to enter. The door latch is on the inside!

We "open the door" to Jesus by acknowledging our sin (see Rom. 3:23) as well as its damaging effects. (See 6:23.) Then we must ask Him to remove that sin from our lives. We do that by confessing it to Him (see 1 John 1:9) in the act of repentance.

Then, believing that His sacrifice on the Cross makes it possible for our sins to be removed (see John 3:16; Rom. 10:9-10), we must also believe that He has completed the work in our own lives. In short, we must reach up in faith—and claim His promises as our own.

The writer of Hebrews nails down the final step of faith in these emphatic words: "Anyone who comes to him must believe that he exists and that he rewards those who earnestly seek him" (11:6).

In short, our commitment to Jesus must be the no-holds-barred kind—total, complete. The result is that each one can become a new person. Paul declares, "If anyone is in Christ, he is a *new* creation; the old has gone, the *new* has come!" (2 Cor. 5:17, emphases added).

---

6. Francis A. Schaeffer, "True Spirituality," clipping with no publication data indicated.

We are wise indeed if we dedicate a lifetime to closely scrutinizing this One who gives us a new lease on life. Let's pause a moment to gaze at a few snapshots from His earthly scrapbook. See Him as He
- stills the raging storm—demonstrating His awesome power
- bids children come and sit on His lap—disclosing His protection of the weak and powerless
- remains silent before Pilate—showing His reaction to attack
- prays in the Garden of Gethsemane—revealing His total obedience to God

After contemplating these, many of us are tempted to say to ourselves: *We can never hope to be all that Jesus was. He fulfilled numerous Old Testament prophecies. He was the very Son of God, who was present at the time of humanity's creation.*

Napoleon spoke the truth when he concluded, "I know men. And Jesus was more than a man."

But, as perfect as He was, our Lord is still within our reach—or, better said, *we're* in *His* reach. Though, of course, we can never *be* Christ, we can *do* things that He did, such as feeding the hungry, comforting the bereaved, confronting the powerful, or teaching God's Word in simple words.

Furthermore, once we commit our hearts to Him, we'll sense a surge of strength within. As Paul put it, we'll be "strengthened with all power according to his glorious might so that you may have great endurance and patience" (Col. 1:11).

For these reasons, Jesus is first and foremost the genesis of our commitment. It all begins with Him, but it certainly doesn't end there. After fully committing ourselves to Him, we'll find that other important commitments come spontaneously.

Let's look at two types of commitment that God highly values.

Commitment to People, Our Special Mission

Mother Teresa stated that the world's worst disease isn't leprosy or tuberculosis. In her words, "The greatest evil is the lack of love and charity, the terrible indifference toward one's neighbor who lives at the roadside assaulted by exploitation, corruption, poverty, and disease."[7]

All of us, even Christians, are prone to get sucked up in the speed, technology, and craziness of the age—at the expense of revealing such love. Virginia Brasier puts it this way:

7. Ted W. Engstrom, *The Fine Art of Friendship* (Nashville: Thomas Nelson Publishers, 1985), 68.

Times of the Mad Atom

This is the age
Of the half-read page.
And the quick hash
And the mad dash.
The bright night
With the nerves tight.
The plane hop
With the brief stop.
The lamp tan
In a short span.
The big Shot
In a good spot.
And the brain strain
And the heart pain.
And the cat naps
Till the spring snaps—
And the fun's done![8]

But even those of us who make time for commitments to persons often fail. And, as Lewis Smedes says, it is often for the same reason.

We commit too quickly. We commit to a relationship before we (or the other person) are mature. We commit unrealistic expectations. We commit while "drunk" with romantic love. We commit with a wretched self-image. We commit without knowing how to effectively communicate.[9]

Perhaps our most grievous fault lies in committing in a manipulative sort of way. We commit not as *givers*, but rather as *takers*—though we're often clever at concealing our intention.

Two biblical ideals guide us in our commitments with others. First, as Christians, our commitment to others must involve generous doses of *submission*. Peter talks about not repaying evil for evil and not snapping back at those who say unkind things. Rather, we must "try to live in peace even if [we] must run after it to catch and hold it!" (1 Pet. 3:11, TLB).

Such commitment leaves us vulnerable to abuse. Peter acknowledges this. But hear his response: "Usually no one will hurt you for wanting to do good. But even if they should, you are to be envied, for God will reward you for it. Quietly trust yourself to Christ your Lord" (vv. 13-15, TLB).

---

8. *Saturday Evening Post*, May 28, 1949, 72. Used with permission of *Saturday Evening Post*, © 1949.

9. Smedes, *Caring and Commitment*, 77.

Then meditate on this final tag line: "Remember, if God wants you to suffer, it is better to suffer for doing good than for doing wrong!" (v. 17, TLB).

Submission must be seen for what it is: a win-win situation.

This principle works even in athletics. Paul "Bear" Bryant rose from working as an Arkansas plowman to become the winningest coach in the history of United States college football. Listen to his secret:

> I have learned how to hold our University of Alabama team together. How to lift some men up, how to calm down others, until finally they have one heartbeat together, a team. There are just three things I would ever say:
> If anything goes bad, *I* did it.
> If anything goes semi-good, then *we* did it.
> If anything goes real good, then *they* did it.[10]

Giving credit to others, accepting blame, not insisting on rights, never seeking revenge—that's what God's Word means by submission.

One final suggestion: Our commitment to others must include doling out a surplus of *encouragement.* As stated previously, the term implies infusing another with courage.

The fifth chapter of 1 Thessalonians has much to say about this imperative (vv. 11-18). Consider this a "checklist for encouragers":

Submission means "voluntarily cooperating with anyone out of love and respect for God [and] for that person." Submitting to nonbelievers is difficult but is vital to leading them to Jesus—though we're never called to disobey God. Submission has these four dimensions:

- functional—distinguishing our roles and the work we do
- relational—loving acknowledgment of another's values
- reciprocal—mutual, humble cooperation with another
- universal—acknowledgment by the Church of the all-encompassing lordship of Jesus.

—*Life Application Study Bible,* s.v. "submission." Copyright © 1988, by Tyndale House Publishers, Inc., Wheaton, Illinois 60189. All rights reserved. Used by permission.

Verse	Example	Suggested Application
11	Build each other up.	Point out to someone a quality you appreciate in him or her.
12	Give honor to leaders.	Look for ways to cooperate.
13	Think highly of leaders.	Withhold your next critical comment.

---

10. Engstrom, *Fine Art of Friendship,* 112.

13	Give wholehearted love to leaders.	Say "thank you" to leaders for their efforts.
13	Avoid quarreling.	Search for ways to get along.
14	Warn the lazy.	Challenge someone to join you in a project.
14	Comfort the frightened.	Remind them of God's promises.
14	Care for the weak.	Love and pray for them.
14	Practice patience.	Recall situations that try your patience; then plan ahead as to how you'll stay calm.
15	Resist revenge.	Overwhelm enemies with kindness.
16	Be joyful.	In the midst of turmoil, remember that God is in control
17	Pray continuously.	God is always with you—talk to Him.
18	Be thankful.	Make a list of God's gifts; thank Him for each one.[11]

Submission. Encouragement. Let's commit ourselves to ministering to others by obeying these biblical admonitions. They require great courage on our part, but we can be assured of this: God is eager to provide an ample supply.

There is, however, one more kind of commitment. It is essential, though often slighted.

Commitment to Principles, Our Means of Obedience

In our day we seem to be obsessed with finding a low-demand gospel, one guaranteed never to inconvenience nor to produce burdensome convictions. And why not? Everything from soft drinks to peaches seems to be going "lite."

With a serious point to make with this humor, one person contrasts "heavy" and "light" religion in these manners:

| Heavy | Light |
| bulky black Bibles with words of Jesus in red | a version that translates Nebuchadnezzar, Zerubbabel, and Jezebel as Waylon, Willie, and Dolly |

---

11. *Life Application Study Bible*, s.v. 1 Thess. 5:11-23. Copyright © 1988, by Tyndale House Publishers, Inc., Wheaton, Illinois 60189. All rights reserved. Used by permission.

knowing doctrines like the Atonement and redemption	simplifying systematic theology into a triune formula: KNOW *yourself*, LOVE *yourself*, BE *yourself*
a day of fasting	skipping breakfast when you're in a hurry, or grabbing a salad bar lunch instead of your usual Whopper
an all-night prayer vigil	a few minutes of "prayer and share"
seven deadly sins	seven minutes with God[12]

His conclusion: "On second thought, perhaps we don't need to lighten the gospel. Maybe we just need to digest the one we've got."[13]

R. V. G. Tasker, former New Testament professor at the University of London, pulls no punches when he declares, "As disciples [we] are called to be a moral disinfectant in a world where moral standards are low, constantly changing or non-existent."[14]

That means one thing: We must not opt for a "lite" gospel. Rather, we're called to an uncompromised obedience to biblical principles.

Unfortunately, many of us seem preoccupied with this question: How close can we come to this world's sordid values and still be Christians? With such an attitude, we're apt to fall prey to the demons of humanism, secularism, intellectualism, and materialism. The result? Eventually our faith is severely diluted—or completely evaporated.

What must we do? God's Word is adamant in proclaiming that we must respond in two ways.

First, we must take protective measures. Let's not kid ourselves—Satan "prowls around like a roaring lion looking for someone to devour" (1 Pet. 5:8).

Furthermore, sin is an ever present, subtle temptation that is regressive in its nature. The first psalm spells out the steps of that regression: "Blessed is the man who does not *walk* in the counsel of the wicked or *stand* in the way of sinners or *sit* in the seat of mockers" (v. 1, emphases added).

Allow me to interpret. When we stop "run[ning] with perseverance the race marked out for us . . . fix[ing] our eyes on Jesus" (Heb. 12:1-2), our hearts begin to gravitate toward evil. At first we walk—and catch a closer

---

12. "Eutychus and His Kin," *Christianity Today*, September 21, 1984, 6. "Eutychus" is a pseudonym.
13. Ibid.
14. Charles R. Swindoll, *Improving Your Serve* (Waco, Tex.: Word, 1981), 132-33.

look at sin's enticements. Soon we're likely to stand in sin's environment—longing to become full participants. Finally, we take our seat among those who relish sinful living. And it all occurs so rapidly, just like riding a descending escalator.

What does this imply? Plainly and simply, it means that we must avoid participation in evil activities, in questionable environments, with sinful persons. To fail to do so is to invite entrapment.

Paul puts it in these emphatic words from God: "Come out from them and be separate, says the Lord. Touch no unclean thing, and I will receive you" (2 Cor. 6:17).

There should be no slowing down to have a better look or to touch. We must keep sprinting for the "prize" (Phil. 3:14). Something seems to be occurring among many believers that concerns me greatly. As they attempt to attract and be attractive to sinners in order to lure them into the Church, believers are becoming full participants in the sinners' value systems and lifestyles.[15] It is plain to see that the secular world has become their model. For example, their religious music reflects the world's beat—and is presented with Hollywood choreography. Theology is made to sound more like contemporary psychology. Standards of behavior and ethics are loosened and eventually ignored.

The idea of these Christians is to stand for little (or for most everything the world stands for) so that outsiders feel less alienated.

At best, their approach is wimpish. At worst, it is downright deceptive—that is, unless these people really no longer stand for much of anything. In that case, unfortunately, they're being sincere.

The truth is this: We must stand for biblical principles, which are fleshed out in personal convictions. These kinds of personal convictions may make us seem a little different to some people—though in ways not intended either to impress or offend.

What are your convictions? Allow me to share a few of mine, most of which, I feel, are grounded as much in social scientific rationale as in biblical principle.

1. I deeply resent the name of God being used in a casual or disrespectful manner. His name is too wonderful to be taken in vain.
2. I consider all forms of gambling—from grocery store lottery to Vegas slot machines—to be an affront to our Heavenly Father.

---

15. See Jon Johnston, *Will Evangelicalism Survive Its Own Popularity?* (Grand Rapids: Zondervan Publishing House, 1980).

Ready for a few more? Here goes:

3. I feel that you always "lose with booze." Given the effects of alcohol in our society, I believe Christians should completely refrain.
4. I maintain that an uncompromising stand must be taken against pornography—whether it appears on the printed page, in the cinema, on videotapes, on television, or via the Internet.
5. I deeply resent racial slurs, even in jest. Our national track record is too pathetic to indulge in such innuendos.

Except for those behaviors expressly stated (by word or principle) in Scripture, I would not expect all of us to agree with my convictions. And that's as it should be, for convictions are tailor-made to our individual walk with Christ.

The key issue is *not* so much whether certain convictions are right; rather, it's whether we have adopted *any* for ourselves. Have we committed ourselves to doing, or refraining from doing, certain things in order to live closer to Christ?

Please understand—I'm certainly not advocating any salvation by works. The holier-than-thou mentality is a turnoff to God and others.

Nevertheless, God does measure our love, in part, by our obedience. (See John 15:10, 14.) One key way we obey is by accepting certain convictions—as His Spirit and His Word sensitize our minds and hearts.

Question: Are there guidelines to follow in choosing certain courses of action? Absolutely. I've found it extremely helpful to ask these nine questions, taken from chapters 9—10 of the Book of 1 Corinthians:

The use of alcoholic beverages wreaks more havoc than perhaps any other facet of our culture. Over two-thirds of the homicides, divorces, automobile accidents, and suicides in the United States are related to alcohol consumption. Some would say, "The Bible does not explicitly prohibit drinking—though it condemns drunkenness." My response: "Neither does the Bible condemn heroin." God's Word gives us timeless principles to apply to our times. Today, unlike in biblical times, alcoholism is a social problem of grave dimensions.

It has been said that a person's name is his or her most valuable possession. In biblical times, people were given names that implied specific traits. When a person changed, frequently his or her name was changed (for example, Saul became Paul). God's name and nature are synonymous. (See Ps. 8:1.) That's why His name is to be hallowed and revered. Jews even refused to pronounce His name. Today we not only say His name but often do so in an irreverent manner. Each time we do so, we are, in effect, insulting His person.

- Does it help my witness for Christ? (9:19-22)
- Am I motivated by a desire to help others know Christ? (9:22-23)
- Does it help me do my best? (9:25)
- Is it against a specific command in Scripture, and thus, sin? (10:12)
- Is it best and helpful? (10:23, 33)
- Am I thinking only of myself, or do I truly care about the other people involved? (10:24)
- Am I acting lovingly or selfishly? (10:28-31)
- Does it glorify God? (10:31)
- Will it encourage someone else to sin? (10:32)[16]

It all really comes down to choices of commitment. Which activities deserve our time, money, and energy priorities? We all need to honestly respond to this pivotal issue on a daily basis.

There is a second way we must respond to biblical principles. *Since we're involved in a battle, we must be more than protective—we must become assertive.*

To refrain from sin is commendable, but we must also challenge evil, take the initiative, go on the offensive, just as our Lord did when He faced up to the lynch mob that attempted to annihilate the adulterous woman, or the money changers who tried to desecrate His Father's Temple.

We must emerge from our tidy and smug religious cocoons to take important stands. Many of us do. The rest of us must do more than applaud—we must join in.

The antiabortion and antipornography efforts have received the most publicity. But other critical battles must be waged, such as

- boycotting products whose companies prey on the helpless in third world countries—their people, their resources
- responding to AIDS victims in a loving, nonjudgmental manner—and challenging other Christians to do likewise
- actively campaigning for qualified candidates who share our biblical perspective
- following our Lord's example by joining in the battle to defend the powerless and victimized—the aged, imprisoned, orphaned, famished

We need not look far to find causes that are near to the heart of God, where the forces of evil and good are engaged. And once we locate the bat-

---

16. *Life Application Study Bible,* s.v. "choices." Copyright © 1988, by Tyndale House Publishers, Inc., Wheaton, Illinois 60189. All rights reserved. Used by permission.

tlefield, we must not be timid about—as the hymn says—"join[ing] in the battle for truth" (Howard B. Grose).

It's time to begin playing march music, readying our weapons, getting a good reading on the enemy, and, most of all, allowing the Lord to fill us with His courage.

Grasp the imagery in this command in Ephesians: "Finally, be strong in the Lord and in his mighty power. Put on the full armor of God so you can take your stand against the devil's schemes. For our struggle is not against flesh and blood, but against the rulers, against the authorities, against the powers of this dark world and against the spiritual forces of evil in the heavenly realms" (6:10-12).

A couple of facts should be disclosed about our spiritual warfare. First, the battle is not easy. Second, it demands that we not become too entrenched in the affairs of this world. Paul says: "Endure hardship . . . like a good soldier of Christ Jesus. No one serving as a soldier gets involved in civilian affairs—he wants to please his commanding officer" (2 Tim. 2:3-4).

Be assured, however, that the victory is well worth the sacrifice. It's really His battle. And as strange as it may seem, it's already won!

Guard Dogs, Graffiti, and True Grit

A son of a coal miner in a family of eight—without the privileges of education—this describes a man who went on to minister for 48 years. The last 23 years of his life, from age 54 to 77, were spent deep in the inner-city area of Los Angeles. I never knew a more committed Christian. He loved Jesus so much that I've seen the very mention of His name bring tears to his eyes. As for his parishioners and community, he loved them. He cared for their sick, counseled their troubled, and cautioned their sinful.

One night he came home without his socks. He had given them to a drifter whose feet were cold. I recall his picketing against the gambling casinos, which were threatening to invade the city. He knew that anguish would follow.

His earthly payoff? He was repeatedly assaulted. His house was robbed. His church was vandalized so many times that he had a guard dog on the premises. How ironic—a dog guarding the house of God!

Toward the end of his ministry, the city cited him as "Man of the Year." He was made official chaplain of his town. He seemed unimpressed, for he looked forward to a far greater and more lasting reward.

This faithful servant "retired" to spend his last two years establishing a ministry in nursing homes. One day, with sadness in his eyes, he said to me, "I heard that they bulldozed my little church. They couldn't find anyone willing to become the pastor." My heart suffered with his.

Then it happened. One day he slumped in his chair with a stroke. They took him to the hospital—with a delirious mind and confused speech.

But somehow his love for Jesus was so ingrained in his inner being that he repeated these words to the doctors: "Praise the Lord." Then, to their amazement, he began to softly sing "We Shall Overcome."

Next to Jesus, this man has influenced my life more than any other. I saw his faithfulness without applause, his obedience without earthly reward, his courage without much acclaim.

Perfect? Far from it. A saint? He would be very uncomfortable being called one. I think I did hear him refer to himself as a beggar who went about telling other beggars where to find bread—the Bread of Life.

I had the privilege of tasting some of that bread. You see, that man was my father. His commitment to the principles of courage provides an excellent example of what it means to stand strong in the face of fear.

12

HOUND DOGS AND OTHER SUCKERS
COURAGE IS LOYALTY

Buddy: "What could be worse than unanswered questions?"
Mensch: "Unquestioned answers."
—"Mensch" comic strip

Genius is the infinite capacity for taking life by the scruff of the neck.
—Christopher Quill

As with birds and insects, God designs our wings to match our weights. His help is
sufficient for our burdens.
—Robert Schuller

Some time ago I read a true story by Suhail Hanna that I can still hardly comprehend. Allow me to share it.

World War II was at its height. Forces were engaged in what was known as the Battle of the Bulge—or the Christmas War of 1944. The fighting was fierce in the bitter cold snow.

The Allied forces bombed and established control of a strategic area. The commanding officer turned to several of his men and said, "Sweep across that field, and kill all German soldiers still entrenched in the snow. I want no prisoners. Absolutely none!"

One of the American soldiers selected gives his account of what happened next. "As I walked, I immediately shot and killed two wounded and suffering soldiers." He continues, "Then, suddenly I approached a tall, young guy with a broad Teutonic forehead.

"He was leaning against a tree. He wasn't wounded—simply exhausted. He had no food, no water, no comrades in sight, no ammunition. Fear, fatigue, defeat, and loneliness overwhelmed him. He spoke English with a beautiful vonderful-world-type accent.

129

"When I noticed a little black Bible in his shirt pocket," he reminisces, "we started to talk about Jesus and salvation.

"Wouldn't you know it, that lanky German soldier turned out to be a born-again Christian who deeply loved the Lord.

"I gave him water from my canteen; I even gave him crackers. Then we prayed and read God's Word together. And we wept together too."

His voice began to tremble as tears splashed down his cheeks. His face began to reflect anguish.

"It seems like only yesterday. We stood a foot or so apart as he read a Psalm from his German Bible. Then I read Romans 12 from my King James translation. He showed me a black-and-white picture of his wife and daughter."

The soldier took a deep breath. "You see, in those days I was a young man in my early twenties. I had just graduated from a Christian college in Illinois and hadn't had time to sort out my thoughts on the war.

"Maybe that's why I did what I did.

"I bid my German brother farewell, took several steps away, then returned to the soldier. Romans 13, the 'thou shalt not kill' commandment, the promises of eternal life, the Prince of Peace, the Sunday School distinction between killing and murder, the irrationality of war —all swirled in my mind.

"When the German soldier saw me returning, he bowed his head and closed his eyes in that classic prayer posture.

"Then it happened. I said three crisp sentences that I still repeat once or twice a week when I have nightmares about the war: 'You're a Christian. I am too. See you later.'

"In less than a second, I transformed that defenseless Christian soldier into a corpse."[1]

The Bland Following the Blind

No doubt the young American feared disobeying the orders of his superior. That could have gotten him court-martialed, and disgraced back home. Besides, Christian or not Christian, this German soldier was part of the German war machine—which was attempting to overtake the world.

The American had to follow orders. His commanding officer always knew best. That's what he had been told since boot camp. But inside his

---

1. Suhail Hanna, "Piecemeal Peace," *Eternity*, December 1981, 30. Used by permission.

heart of hearts, he knew what he had done was wrong. His Heavenly Commander did *not* approve.

His loyalty had been a *blind loyalty*, a robotic reflex, a complete disregard for his conscience and better judgment.[2]

Is blind loyalty commendable? Perhaps it is for hound dogs—who learn unquestioned obedience even if it means giving their lives to divert the attention of a 500-pound grizzly bear. But what about people? Should we manifest hound-dog loyalty? Not really, because it allows others to do our thinking and to determine our fate. Then we're forced to live with the nightmarish consequences and to absorb the guilt.

Examine the testimony of the general who ordered Japan's attack on Pearl Harbor. Why did he do it? Blind loyalty.

At a Youth for Christ rally, I once heard this former leader of the Emperor's navy describe the inner turmoil that took place in his heart. Soon after the war, he repented and became a victorious Christian. His underlying message: Blind loyalty isn't enough—not by a long shot.

Essentially, the word "loyalty" means "being faithful to one's allegiance or oath."[3] Loyalty comes in two major forms:

- loyalty that's *imposed on us from another or others* (blind loyalty)
- loyalty that *we impose on ourselves* because of principles we accept as true and trustworthy (convinced loyalty)

Christian courage has little in common with the first of these. However, the second is the natural outgrowth of Christian courage.

Open Eyes, Open Mind, Open Heart

Does our Savior want our loyalty? Absolutely. But only after we've weighed the facts and are convinced in our own minds. Why? Because He wants us to fully understand the cost involved.

Jesus spells out His price in these words: "Anyone who wants to be my follower must love me far more than he does his own father, mother, wife, children, brothers, or sisters—yes, more than his own life—otherwise he cannot be my disciple" (Luke 14:26, TLB).

Then He adds, "And no one can be my disciple who does not carry his own cross and follow me" (v. 27, TLB).

That's something to think about—quite a price to pay. Here's a kind of loyalty that demands tremendous courage and determination. Thus, our

---

2. See chapter 7, which reveals Kohlberg's morality model. It is apparent that blind faith corresponds to stage 4, "law and order." Recall that Kohlberg states that few rise above this stage.

3. *Random House Dictionary*, s.v. "loyalty."

decision must not be impulsive; it must be deliberate and methodically reasoned out.

Jesus says so. After specifying the cost, He recommends carefully weighing the consequences. Like the man who builds a tower: "Will he not first sit down and estimate the cost to see if he has enough money to complete it?" (v. 28). Or like a king going to war: "Will he not first sit down and consider whether he is able with ten thousand men to oppose the one coming against him with twenty thousand?" (v. 31).

The point we have established is this: Unlike many cult leaders we've heard about, Jesus does not want us to be blindly loyal to Him. Rather, He wants us to be so convinced that *His* way is *our* way that we'll be eager to take courageous stands. Without that strong inner assurance, we're likely to fall by the wayside.

The truth is that just because we decide on our own whom (or what) we'll be loyal to, that certainly doesn't guarantee that our choices will be wise.

Fool's Gold

Many of us are sorely tempted to give primary allegiance to items of lesser value. Like miners during the days of the California gold rush, we're deceived by a kind of fool's gold. It *looks* authentic—but in reality, it's virtually worthless.

What are some kinds of fool's gold that many of us grasp for?

1. *Job*—For most of us males, our occupations assume top priority. Jobs can be the main basis for our identities and the primary focus of our attention. We're fiercely loyal to bosses and faithful to our job's requirements. I know of one workaholic who has lost his wife, his children, and his sanity.

2. *Family*—As the preceding words of Jesus spell out, our biological kin must be subordinate to our relationship with God. On several occasions He had to explain this to Mary and His brothers. Renowned missionary E. Stanley Jones had to pry himself away from his aged, demanding mother in order to follow God's leading to India. Though close-knit families are a worthy goal, we need to be cautious about allowing them to dominate our loyalties to the exclusion of our loyalty and devotion for God himself.

3. *Money*—Thoughts of money can consume us. Charles Swindoll tells about a West Palm Beach, Florida, woman who died of malnutrition after wasting away to 50 pounds. Investigators found that she lived in a veritable pigpen. She had begged food from neighbors and gone to the Salvation Army for clothes. Amid her belongings, two keys to safe-deposit boxes were

found. The first box held 700 AT&T stock certificates as well as hundreds of securities, bonds, and other valuable certificates—plus $200,000 in cash. The second box contained $600,000 in cash. This woman was a millionaire who died a stark victim of starvation in a humble hovel. To paraphrase another, *She knew the worth of everything, but the value of nothing.*[4]

To these three forms of fool's gold can be added many others: friends, home, cars, celebrities, nature, hobbies, service clubs, sports, and food, to name just a few.

In summary, loyalty is something that should be our choice. Jesus tells us to cautiously weigh options and to make our own decisions. But in choosing, it's imperative that we establish priorities according to His scheme of things.

That means choosing Him, His concerns, His commandments, and His will first. We must be absolutely loyal to these. Though few of us really do this, I'm quite certain that most of us agree on its rightness. But from that point on, the loyalty business can get pretty sticky.

Searching for My Crowd

Don't get me wrong; I'm a joiner like many of the rest of us. I belong to a denomination, professional organizations, the Sheraton Club, and—oh, yes; I almost forgot—I'm a rabid Dodger fan.

The certificates and logos of these organizations are on my walls, on cards in my wallet, and even inscribed on clothes I wear. Yet on second thought, I guess I don't really belong—in the sense that I bury my identity in most of these organizations. That's because some time ago I bought into the belief that only Jesus can control my life without destroying it.

If He is, in actuality, the only One who controls me—if He possesses my primary loyalty—then I don't feel right in allowing myself to be swallowed up by any man-made social body. That's good in a way, because I've never found any one group that I totally agree with. There are always a few places where my own identity and the identity of the group simply don't mesh.

Here's a bird's-eye view of my situation: Though far from being fanatical, I'm fairly conservative in my theology—holding to the absolute authority of God's Word, the divinity of Christ, and even to some personal convictions. But when I talk with other persons who are theologically conservative, I invariably pick up on calloused, "redneck" talk among some of them. I instantly recognize that I cannot identify with these people either. Go ahead

---

4. Swindoll, *Improving Your Serve*, 50.

—color Jon Johnston "liberal" when it comes to nonviolence and believing that we should render compassion.

So in reality I guess I'm hybrid: a conservative liberal or, if you prefer, a liberal conservative. I'm really not at home in either camp.

When I'm tempted to second-guess my stance, which to many may seem inconsistent and counterproductive, I think about some courageous heroes—who just happen to share my basic position. Persons like John Wesley, Chuck Colson, Mother Teresa, Mark Hatfield. And that picks me up better than drinking iced tea.

All of this is to say that our loyalty to organizations must be subordinate to our loyalty to biblical principles. To the extent we're convinced that organizations square with these positions, they merit our loyalty. To the degree they deviate, no matter how worthy they're perceived to be, we should resign from their team.

Taking this kind of position requires a heavy dose of courage—courage that can come only from being inhabited by the very presence of God's Spirit. Why is this so? Because our natural inclinations pull us in the *opposite* direction.

All Tarred with the Same Brush

Calvin Redekop has written a fine book titled *The Free Church and Seductive Culture*. In it he presents four sociological principles that push all of us in the direction of becoming indiscriminate loyalists.

1. *Ethnocentrism principle*—We defend, boost, and identify ourselves with the groups to which we belong. We see things from their perspective. (Contrast a southern Alabama Ku Klux Klan member's perspective with that of a New England member of the American Civil Liberties Union.)

2. *Socialization principle*—We become like persons in our social system. They're our reference group. We continuously compare and contrast ourselves with them. In short, they determine the values, beliefs, and norms that we internalize. (Notice how teenagers seem to talk and dress alike and how they tolerate the same music!)

3. *Reciprocity principle*—We usually don't give something away without receiving something of equal value. Our social networks supply us with power, status, and prestige. We resist the inevitable withdrawal pains that are associated with relinquishing these. Thus, we're likely to remain cemented in our present relationships. (I know someone who despises his church yet would not think of attending another. He has "too much to lose.")

4. *Self-deceiving principle*—We have an uncanny ability to misinterpret and pervert objective reality. We see what we want to see. Our

rose-colored glasses show us a fantasized reality. Thus, many of us are unable to perceive our organizational structures clearly—or judge them objectively.[5] (I once knew someone who was so cantankerous that the only good thing you could say about him was that he was not born a twin! Yet to his mother he was angelic. That's a lack of objectivity.)

To simplify and abbreviate these important principles, we do plenty of mindless flag-waving, conforming, reward hoarding, and rationalizing. Together, these inhibit us from seeing our social involvements as they really are. And they keep us from being willing to refuse them our loyalty.

As Christians, we must not allow our roots to dig down too deeply in organizational structures—whether they be associated with church, family, job, or recreation. Furthermore, we must constantly judge how closely their goals and activities correspond with the teachings in God's Word.

Here's where courage enters the picture. If we detect incongruities between our social networks and His standards, we must bite the bullet and back off from (or find new) social networks.

Is it OK to be loyal to organizations? Sure—once we're sure they'll help, rather than hinder, our walk with God.

A certain amount of loyalty is expected, and even demanded, by the associations we join. In fact, they need it if they're to survive. But, like crabgrass and fingernails, our loyalty must be periodically examined and trimmed back. Otherwise, it's bound to get out of hand.

All Our Loyalty Eggs in One Basket

From the foregoing discussion, we see that loyalty to biblical principles is essential. That implies one conclusion: Our ultimate loyalty must be to Jesus Christ, the Living Word. All other loyalties must be subordinated to (and judged by) that one pivotal loyalty.

Doing that requires a mature spiritual courage—a courage that can come only by relying on His omnipotent power. And that means losing ourselves in Him.

What do we have to gain by submerging our identities in His so that His purposes become ours and His battles also become ours?

The Bible proclaims these rich dividends:

Rom. 3:24   We're declared "not guilty" of sin.

Rom. 8:1   No condemnation awaits us.

Rom. 8:2   We're free from the vicious cycle of sin and death.

---

5. Calvin Redekop, *The Free Church and Seductive Culture* (Philadelphia: Herald Press, 1970), 84-86.

1 Cor. 1:2	We're acceptable to God through Jesus Christ.
1 Cor. 1:30	We're pure and holy.
1 Cor. 15:22	We'll rise again.
2 Cor. 3:17	We're free from trying to be saved by being good.
2 Cor. 5:17	We're brand-new people inside.
2 Cor. 5:21	We're full of God's goodness.
Gal. 3:28	We're one in Christ with all other believers.
Eph. 1:3	We're blessed with every spiritual blessing.
Eph. 1:4	We're holy, faultless, and covered with God's love.
Eph. 1:5-6	We belong to Christ.
Eph. 1:7	Our sins are taken away—we're forgiven.
Eph. 1:10-11	We'll live with Christ forever; we're gifts to God.
Eph. 1:13	We're marked by the Holy Spirit as belonging to God.
Eph. 2:6	We've been lifted from the grave to sit with Christ in glory.
Eph. 2:10	We've been given new lives.
Eph. 2:13	We've been brought near to God.
Eph. 3:6	We will receive great blessings.
Eph. 3:12	We can come fearlessly into God's presence.
Eph. 5:29-30	We are part of Christ's Body, the Church.
Col. 2:10	We have everything because we have Christ; we are filled with God.
Col. 2:11	We are set free from our evil desires.
2 Tim. 2:10	We will have eternal glory.[6]

Who could ask for anything more? The past is forgiven. The present is meaningful and significant, the future assured. Great payoffs! But best of all, by identifying with Him, we buy into rich, continuous fellowship with Him. And there's no better company—anywhere!

Perhaps it's under conditions of persecution that we achieve our closest intimacy with, and greatest loyalty to, the Savior. One man convinced me of this. I share his story in the following section.

Twenty Mongolian Winters

On a trip to China one year I met a true hero. This man was asked to recant his faith shortly after the Communist Revolution, and he emphatically refused. That earned him a life sentence in a Mongolian prison.

---

6. *Life Application Study Bible*, s.v. "loyalty." Copyright © 1988, by Tyndale House Publishers, Inc., Wheaton, Illinois 60189. All rights reserved. Used by permission.

After nearly 21 years, at age 65, he was released and put under house arrest in Beijing. Someone put us in contact, and I had the rare opportunity to converse with him about those years of incarceration.

He smiled as he thanked God for helping him to persevere, and for his recent release—which was totally unexpected. He also rejoiced in the converts he had won in the prison. As I remember, some of those converts even included the guards.

His face grimaced, though, as he spoke of the extreme hardship he had to endure. It was beyond belief. Many of his fellow prisoners could not take the abuse and died. But he was somehow able to endure.

I asked that he might offer a word of prayer. His words were electric. His spirit was contagious. His devotion seemed so deep. It was like being in the presence of an Old Testament prophet.

After we prayed, I looked at him and naively said, "I can hardly imagine what you went through. You were literally tortured beyond belief."

Without batting an eye or giving the slightest hint of self-pity, he looked at me and said, "*What I endured was nothing compared to the Crucifixion.*"

Here was a man who so closely identified with our Lord and His sufferings that he purposely compared his ordeal with that of his Master. As a result of his intense loyalty, he simply refused to look back on his extreme trial with bitterness or resentment—or even regret.

Instead, there was a bright note of thanksgiving—thanksgiving for the privilege of sharing in Christ's sufferings (see 1 Pet. 4:13); thanksgiving for his "premature" release—for he had resigned himself to dying there in prison.

With a broad smile, he looked at me and joked, "See here," pointing to his dark head of hair, "God didn't even let my hair go gray!"

For this man, and for all of us who follow Jesus, courage is indeed loyalty to Him and to all He stands for.

And when the cost is weighed against His eternal dividends, we realize that it's indeed a minimal price to pay, even if it must be paid in a Mongolian prison.

Try something. I have, and it's provided a tremendous uplift. The next time your problems seem overwhelming—which could be today—just pause long enough to bow your head and pray these words: *Dear Lord, what I'm enduring is really nothing compared to Your crucifixion.*

A PARTING WORD

I had to smile when I recently encountered this sign:[1]

Lost Dog
3 legs
Blind in left eye
Right ear missing
Tail broken
Accidentally neutered
Answers to name of Lucky

Many of us answer to the name *Courageous*. We relish it when others perceive us in this way. And we like to think of ourselves as stalwarts: indomitable, unyielding, unconquerable, real giant killers!

Why do we want to claim the name *Courageous*? Because from our cradles onward we've learned that courage is a universally acclaimed virtue. It's a badge worn proudly—a virtue that nations, communities, families, and coaches handsomely reward, something that could very likely get us in the Hall of Fame, *Who's Who*, the *Guinness Book of World Records*, or even a history book.

But unfortunately, often our actual characteristics fail to square with our courage tag. We're considered courageous, but in reality it's a clear case of mistaken identity. We know it, because the evidence is indisputable.

We wince, or hide, when faced with a challenge. We're obsessed with our comfort. We duck anything that makes us fearful in the slightest degree. We're so paranoid that even our fears have fears!

In short, we've calculated the cost of true courage, and we're unwilling to pay it.

Please Step to the Cashier

This book maintains that authentic courage is indeed costly—in all of the forms described. It's not something that can be quickly picked up at

---

1. Sign located on wall of J. C. Plumbing store in Thousand Oaks, California. Source unknown.

some bargain basement. It can't be learned in a three-step formula at some weekend seminar, or even acquired from courageous parents.

In a way, becoming courageous is a lot like mastering the violin. I'm reminded of the lady who rushed up to famed violinist Fritz Kreisler after a concert and said, "I'd give my life to play as beautifully as you do."

Kreisler softly replied, "Ma'am, I did."

Courage requires a lifetime of arduous dedication.

Question: What are we dedicating our lives to? Security? The purchase and maintenance of expensive "toys"? Avoidance of conflict? Safety? Presenting a facade to others? Dousing our fears?

Or, by contrast, are our sights fixed on righting wrongs, correcting injustices, shouldering unpopular but worthy causes, or keeping our chins up in the face of the harshest adversities—and all without resentment or regret?

Even these are insufficient from our Christian perspective. Scores of devout humanists, atheists, and secularists sacrificially champion noble causes. And in their eyes, this makes them self-sufficient and even self-righteous. They claim to be better than the average Christian.

Then what is essentially unique about Christian courage?

First, the *source* of Christian courage is God. A favorite verse of mine is "God did not give us a spirit of timidity, but a spirit of power, of love and of self-discipline" (2 Tim. 1:7).

We don't have to work up our nerve or generate enough willpower to be courageous. Rather, Christ entreats us to relinquish our timidity and fear to His care (1 Pet. 5:7) and open our hearts to receive the inner strength He generously provides. How does this come about? Through fervent and sincere prayer—prayer that causes us to look up in faith and expectancy.

Again, for us it's not by effort, but by surrender that we receive our courage. And the supply is always generous.

Second, the *focus* of Christian courage is found in God's reliable Word. It's here where we find those critical issues and attitudes that demand our action. With assurance Paul writes, "All Scripture is God-breathed and is useful for teaching, rebuking, correcting and training in righteousness, so that the man of God may be thoroughly equipped for every good work" (2 Tim. 3:16-17).

Third, the *motivator* of courage is prayer. An old adage goes, "Satan flees when he sees the weakest of us on our knees." Why? Because he knows that by praying we're on our way to becoming bold.

Prayer linkage with God means that our timidity will evaporate, and His promises will become our possessions.

To paraphrase my respected friend Eugene Stowe, prayer does for us what a tuning fork does for a piano. It eliminates discord between us and God so that we're on the right spiritual pitch. And the removal of such discord prompts us to be courageous.[2]

Shrinking Supply, Expanding Demand

As previously stated, courage is more rare than it is plentiful. And many of us believe its supply resembles that of the world's crude oil—it's rapidly diminishing. That's truly tragic—at a time when challenges seem to be growing in number and complexity.

Even a passing glance at what is predicted for the next 100 years sends chills up our spine: acute food and energy shortages, overpopulation, more sophisticated drugs, a worldwide AIDS epidemic that could rival the plague known as the Black Death.

Furthermore, in those pockets where our courage is found, it seems mostly to take the form of maximizing our self-interest, of getting our way so that we're one up on situations or persons, insisting on our rights, pushing our way to acquire increased power, privilege, prestige, possessions. In short, it takes the form of taking care of number one.

Christian courage, by contrast, is directed toward *obeying* God's Word and serving others. It's directed toward giving rather than getting and toward holiness rather than personal happiness.

How is this possible? Again, the presence of His Spirit within our hearts gently pulls us in this direction—if we're totally dependent on Him.

Even when suffering is required—as it often is—we won't flinch, at least not for long. Why? Because we know that we *share in his [Christ's] sufferings in order that we may also share in his glory* (Rom. 8:17). We valiantly identify with the pain of our Lord, who endured the Cross for us. (See 1 Pet. 4:12-13.)

Stake-driving Time

In the Old West of the United States, people finalized decisions about property lines with stakes. Once driven into the earth, marking where one's property stopped and another's began, all turmoil and indecision was supposed to cease. The boundary was proclaimed as official.

We need to drive the "courage stake" deeply into the ground—once we've carefully weighed the options. It comes down to a critical choice that

---

2. Stated by Eugene Stowe, then chairman of the Board of General Superintendents, Church of the Nazarene, at the Anaheim District Church of the Nazarene Retreat, November 1989.

we must all make. Will we be sedentary, "settler" believers—deeply entrenched in our ways? Will we be immobile, traditional to a fault? Or will we be dynamic, "pioneer" Christians—adventuresome, ever hopeful, flexible, risk taking, courageous?

To borrow my wife's term, will we be "pew potatoes" or daring, challenge-seeking believers? We must make this choice.

George Bernard Shaw puts his finger on the crux in this convicting statement:

> This is the true joy in life, the being used for a purpose recognized by yourself as a mighty one: the being thoroughly worn-out before you are thrown on the scrap heap, and being a force of nature instead of a feverish selfish little clod of ailments and grievances, complaining that the world will not devote itself to making you happy.

Question: Once our stake is driven, will our fears somehow evaporate like midday Malibu fog? Hardly. Problems, difficult people, and heart-thumping trepidation will stalk our paths until we get to heaven.

Nevertheless, in the face of such fears, we can stand tall. As Christians, we have a coping mechanism that nonbelievers lack—a sound, reliable courage that expands as our challenges grow. As Annie Johnson Flint's song says, "He giveth more grace when the burdens grow greater."

Down deep, almost all of us desire to live a significant life. We see too many around us who, as Henry David Thoreau said, live lives of "quiet desperation"—treading water, being restless, always anticipating the next stage. Alienated.

We truly hope that our earthly existence can be different. We want to count for something, to have purpose—rather than being just a temporary configuration of atoms.

In no way does that mean we desire to have statues erected in our memories. We just want to be able to say at life's end, "My life was worth living. Things are at least slightly better in the world because I was here."

And there's no way to escape this conclusion. To be able to say this requires taking courageous stands. Through His power. For His purpose. With His people. In spite of opposition.

Now please understand: standing up for eternal values does not preclude other normal activities. We need not grow a beard, move to the desert, and meditate 20 hours a day. Perhaps the world has too many religious eccentrics already.

Rather, we must in our world align our priorities with God's Word and remember to keep Jesus at the center.

Paul made tents, Calvin practiced law, Milton wrote poetry, Pascal was a mathematician, Dorothy Sayers wrote mysteries, Mother Hale took care of Harlem babies. But all took (or take) courageous stands for Jesus.[3]

Focusing on the eternal is bound to lead us more deeply into the world—working for justice for the powerless, bringing healing to the wounded, offering forgiveness to the guilty.

Then, when our life draws to an end, we'll rest assured that we've truly made a significant difference all because of Jesus at work within us. And nothing seems more important.

I came upon the following statement by the eminent philosopher Søren Kierkegaard, who wrote over 100 years ago. Weigh it carefully. Personalize it. Seriously contemplate its truth.

> One lives only once. If when death comes the life is well spent, that is, spent so that it is related rightly to eternity—then God be praised eternally. If not, then it is irremediable—one only lives once.[4]

Will we give God the permission to begin calling us "courageous"? Then, with His constant help, will we *be* courageous—even in the smallest details of our lives?

We must do so. Our fears must never get the best of us. Never!

---

3. Daniel Taylor, "The Fear of Insignificance," *Christianity Today*, February 3, 1989, 26.
4. Ibid.